BERLITZ

HUNGARIAN
FOR TRAVELLERS

By the staff of Editions Berlitz

Library of Congress Catalog Card Number: 02-799880-0

1st printing

Printed in Switzerland

Berlitz Trademark Reg. U.S. Patent Office
and other countries—Marca Registrada

Editions Berlitz
1, avenue des Jordils
1000 Lausanne 6, Switzerland

Preface

You are about to visit Hungary. Our aim has been to produce a practical phrase book to help you on your trip.

In preparing this book we took into account a wealth of suggestions from phrase book users around the world. The accent is on helping the traveller in practical, every-day situations.

The contents are logically arranged so you can find the right phrase at the moment you need it.

Hungarian for Travellers features:

- all the phrases and supplementary vocabulary you'll need on your trip
- complete phonetic transcription throughout, enabling you to pronounce every word correctly
- special panels showing replies your listener might like to give you: just hand him the book and let him point to the appropriate phrase. This is particularly useful in certain difficult situations (trouble with the car, at the doctor's, etc.)
- a wide range of travel facts, hints and useful practical information, providing a valuable insight into life in Hungary
- a tipping chart (see inside back-cover) and a reference section in the back of the book
- an introduction to some basics of Hungarian grammar

Certain sections will be particularly appreciated by travellers: the extensive "Eating Out" chapter which explains what's on the menu, in the soup and under the sauce, with translations, and the complete "Shopping Guide" which enables you to be almost as specific and selective as you would be at home. Trouble with the car? Turn to the mechanic's manual with its dual-language terms. Feeling ill? Our medical section provides the most rapid communication possible between you and the doctor.

To make the most of *Hungarian for Travellers*, we suggest that you start with the "Guide to Pronunciation". Then go on to "Some Basic Expressions". This not only gives you a minimum vocabulary, it also helps you get used to pronouncing the language.

We are particularly grateful to Mr. David Pulman and Mr. Norbert Urban for their help in the preparation of this book, and to Dr. T.J.A. Bennett who devised the phonetic transcription system. We also wish to extend special thanks to Vue Touristique I.P.V., Budapest, and to Prof. Joseph J. Hollos for their decisive roles in guiding this project to fruition.

We shall be very pleased to receive any comments, criticisms and suggestions that you think may help uns in preparing future editions.

Have a good trip.

Throughout this book the symbols illustrated here indicate sections containing phrases your listener might like to say to *you*. If you don't understand him, just give him the book and let him point to the phrase in his language. The English translation is just beside.

A very basic grammar

Hungarian is a unique, intricate, subtle language belonging to the Finno-Ugric family.* It's completely unrelated to Slavonic, Germanic or any other Indo-European tongue.

Hungarian words are highly derivative, various ideas and nuances being expressed by a root-word modified in different ways. Instead of prepositions ("to", "from", "in", etc.), Hungarian uses a variety of suffixes (tags added to the ends of words) to achieve the same effect. Special endings are also added to verbs, pronouns and other parts of speech. The choice of suffix is partly governed by a complicated set of rules of vowel harmony. What this means is that the vowels in the root-word determine which alternative of the required suffix must be added.

Take a stab at the suffix

In some phrases in this book we have had no alternative but to leave the choice of suffix open, since it depends on the word you wish to insert in front of it. It's impossible for us to give here a watertight summary of the technicalities of vowel harmony. However, if you follow the rules of thumb given below you'll considerably shorten the odds on picking the correct suffix.

- If the basic word is dominated by "open" vowels (**e, é, i, í, ö, ő, ü, ű**), add that suffix which also contains an "open" vowel.

- If the basic word is dominated by "closed" vowels (**a, á, o, ó, u, ú**), add that suffix which also contains a "closed" vowel.

Don't worry about making a mistake, you'll be understood—and most likely complimented for trying hard!

---

* Its closest, yet still extremely distant, relative is Finnish.

Articles

1. **Definite article** (the):

The word for *the* is **a** before a word beginning with a consonant, and **az** before a vowel, in both singular and plural. It is indeclinable.

singular		plural	
a vonat	the train	**a vonatok**	the trains
az asztal	the table	**az asztalok**	the tables

2. **Indefinite article** (a/an):

The indefinite article is always **egy** (the same as the word for "one"). It is indeclinable.

egy vonat	a train	**egy asztal**	a table

Nouns

As in English, there is no grammatical gender. However, nouns take various endings depending on their case.

Here is a general model of the declension of nouns based on the word **könyv** (book), showing the endings to be added. Note, however, that endings are often subject to change according to the rules of vowel harmony.

case	singular	plural	usage
subject	**könyv**	**könyvek**	the book(s) (is/are ...)
dir. obj.	**könyveket**	**könyveket**	(I read) the book(s)
possess.	**könyvnek a**	**könyveknek a**	of the book(s)
ind. obj.	**könyvnek**	**könyveknek**	to the book(s)
place	**könyvben**	**könyvekben**	in the book(s)
"from"	**könyvről**	**könyvekről**	from the book(s)

GRAMMAR

Adjectives

1. The adjective precedes the noun, with no endings.

a piros autó   the red car   **a piros autók**   the red cars

2. The comparative of an adjective is formed by adding the endings **-bb**, **-abb**, **-ebb** or **-obb** to its simple form.

3. In the superlative, the adjective takes the same endings but is also preceded by **leg**. Here are some useful examples.

simple	comparative	superlative
jó good	**jobb** better	**legjobb** best
magas tall	**magasabb** taller	**legmagasabb** tallest
szép beautiful	**szebb** more beautiful	**legszebb** most beautiful
nagy big	**nagyobb** bigger	**legnagyobb** biggest

Personal pronouns

subject		direct object (me, etc.)	indirect object (to me, etc.)
I	**én**	**engem**	**nekem**
you	**maga***	**magát***	**magának***
you	**te**	**téged**	**neked**
he / she / it	**ő**	**őt**	**neki**
we	**mi**	**minket**	**nekünk**
you	**maguk***	**magukat***	**maguknak***
you	**ti**	**titeket**	**nektek**
they	**ők**	**őket**	**nekik**

* Polite form for "you".

GRAMMAR

Demonstratives

this **ez**   these **ezek**   that **az**   those **azok**

Possessives

To form the possessive case, take the definite article + the personal pronoun + the noun. The noun takes endings (again, governed by a complicated set of rules).

my book	**az én könyvem**	our book	**a mi könyvünk**	
your book	**a maga könyve***	your book	**a maguk könyve***	
your book	**a te könyved**	your book	**a mi könyvünk**	
his/her book	**az ő könyve**	their book	**az ő könyvük**	

Verbs

Because of the complexity of Hungarian verbs we have restricted ourselves to showing how to form the present and future tenses of verbs, including the special cases of the verbs "to be" and "to have".

1. Present tense of the verbs "to be" and "to have":

to be (**lenni**)			
I am	**én vagyok**	we are	**mi vagyunk**
you are	**maga van***	you are	**maguk vannak***
you are	**te vagy**	you are	**ti vagytok**
he/she/it is	**ő van**	they are	**ők vannak**

to have (**vanéki**)			
I have	**nekem van**	we have	**nekünk van**
you have	**magának van***	you have	**maguknak van***
you have	**neked van**	you have	**nektek van**
he/she/it has	**neki van**	they have	**nekik van**

---

* Polite form for "you", "your".

2. Present tense of other verbs:

The present tense may be formed in various ways. Here is a common pattern for transitive verbs (i.e. those which can take a direct object) based on the infinitive **olvasni** (to read).

I read	én olvasom	we read	mi olvassuk
you read	maga olvassa*	you read	maguk olvassák*
you read	te olvasod	you read	ti olvassátok
he/she reads	ő olvassa	they read	ők olvassák

Questions: **olvassa ő?** = does he/she read? etc.

3. Future

A simple method of forming the future tense is to use the personal pronoun + the word corresponding to "shall" or "will" (**fogok/fogsz**, etc.) + the infinitive. Here we take the verb **vásárolni** (to shop) as an example (I shall shop/go shopping, etc.).

I ...	én fogok vásárolni	we ...	mi fogunk vásárolni
you ...	maga fog vásárolni*	you ...	maguk fognak vásárolni*
you ...	te fogsz vásárolni	you ...	ti fogtok vásárolni
he/she ...	ő fog vásárolni	they ...	ők fognak vásárolni

Negatives

In a sentence, the word **nem** is usually placed after the subject. There is also a change of word order (inversion).

| I am here | **én itt vagyok** |
| I am not here | **én nem vagyok itt** |

---

* Polite form for "you".

GRAMMAR

Guide to pronunciation

This and the following chapter are intended to make you familiar with the phonetic transcription we devised and to help you get used to the sounds of Hungarian.

As a minimum vocabulary for your trip, we've selected a number of basic words and phrases under the title "Some Basic Expressions" (pages 16–21).

An outline of the spelling and sounds of Hungarian

You'll find the pronunciation of the Hungarian letters and sounds explained below, as well as the symbols we use for them in the transcription. Note that Hungarian has some diacritical signs—special markings over certain letters—which we don't use in English.

The imitated pronunciation should be read as if it were English except for any special rules set out below. It is based on Standard British pronunciation, though we have tried to take into account General American pronunciation as well. Of course, the sounds of any two languages are never exactly the same; but if you follow carefully the indications supplied here, you'll have no difficulty in reading our transcription in such a way as to make yourself understood.

Letters written in **bold** type should be stressed (pronounced louder).

Consonants

Letter	Approximate pronunciation	Symbol	Example
b, d, f, h, m, n, v, x, z	as in English		
c	like **ts** in ne**ts**	ts	**arc** orts

PRONUNCIATION

cs	like **ch** in **ch**ap	ch	**kocsi**	**kaw**chee
g	always as in **g**o, never as in **g**in	g/gh	**gáz** **régi**	**gaaz** **ray**ghee
gy	like **di** in me**di**um, said fairly quickly	dʸ	**ágy**	aadʸ
j	like **y** in **y**es	y/ʸ	**jég**	**y**ayg
k	always as in si**ck**, never as in **k**ill	k	**kör**	**k**urr
l	always as in **l**eap, never as in ba**ll**	l	**ital**	**ee**tol
ly	like **y** in **y**es	y/ʸ	**Károly**	**kaa**rawʸ
ny	quite like **ni** in o**ni**on	nʸ	**hány**	**haan**ʸ
p	always as in si**p**, never as in **p**ill	p	**posta**	**paw**shto
r	pronounced with the tip of the tongue, like Scottish **r**	r	**ír**	**ēē**r
s	like **sh** in **sh**oot	sh	**saláta**	**sh**ollaato
sz	like **s** in **s**o	s/ss	**szó** **ész**	**saw** **ayss**
t	always as in si**t**, never as in **t**ill	t	**túra**	**tōō**ro
ty	quite like **tti** in pre**tti**er, said quickly	tʸ	**atya**	otʸo
zs	like **s** in plea**s**ure	zh	**zsír**	**zhēē**r

Vowels

a	quite like **o** in n**o**t (British pronunciation)	o	**hat**	h**o**t
á	like **a** in c**a**r, but without any r-sound	aa	**rág**	r**aa**g
e	quite like **e** in y**e**s, but with the mouth a little more open, i.e. a sound between **e** in y**e**s and **a** in h**a**t	æ	**te**	t**æ**
é	like **ay** in s**ay**, but a pure vowel, not a diphthong, i.e. neither the tongue nor the lips move during the pronunciation of it	ay	**mér**	m**ay**r

i	like **ee** in f**ee**t (short)	ee	**hideg**	**heed**æg
í	like **ee** in s**ee** (long)	e͞e	**míg**	**m**e͞e**g**
	quite like **aw** in s**aw** (British pronunciation), but shorter	aw	**bot**	**bawt**
ó	like **aw** in s**aw**, but with the tongue higher in the mouth	a͞w	**fotó**	**fawt**a͞w
ö	like **ur** in f**ur**, but short, without any r-sound, and with rounded lips	ur	**örök**	**ur**rurk
ő	like **ur** in f**ur**, but without any r-sound, and with the lips tightly rounded	u͞r	**lő**	**l**u͞r
u	as in the British pronunciation of p**u**ll	oo	**kulcs**	**koo**lch
ú	like **oo** in f**oo**d	o͞o	**kút**	**k**o͞o**t**
ü	a "rounded **ee**"; while pronouncing **ee** as in s**ee**, round your lips as if to pronounce **oo** as in s**oo**n; the resulting sound should be as in French **u**ne or German f**ü**nf	ew	**körül**	**ku**rrewl
ű	the same sound as **ü**, but long and with the lips more tightly rounded	e͞w	**fűt**	**f**e͞w**t**

PRONUNCIATION

N.B. 1) There are no "silent" letters in Hungarian, so all letters must be pronounced. This means that double consonants are pronounced long, e.g. **tt** in kettő (**kæt-t**u͞r) sounds rather like **t-t** in a fast pronunciation of part-time. (But a double consonant appearing at the end of a word is pronounced short). It also means that vowels standing next to each other are pronounced separately and do not combine to produce diphthongs.

2) When two or more consonants stand next to each other, the last one can influence the pronunciation of the others. If it is "voiceless", it will make a preceding "voiced" consonant into a "voiceless" one, and vice versa, e.g. *végtelen* is

pronounced as if it were written *véktelen*. The "voiceless" consonants are **c**, **f**, **k**, **p**, **s**, **sz**, **t**, **ty**, and the corresponding "voiced" ones are **dz**, **v**, **g**, **b**, **zs**, **z**, **d**, **gy**.

3) Every word, when pronounced alone, has a strong stress on its first syllable. When words are combined in sentences, the stress on the less important words weakens.

4) The "double" forms of **cs**, **gy**, **ly**, **ny**, **sz**, **ty**, **zs** are **ccs**, **ggy**, **lly**, **nny**, **ssz**, **tty**, **zzs**. If the "double" form is divided at the end of a line, then the single form is written twice, e.g. **cs-cs** instead of **c-cs**.

5) In Hungarian, the letter **j** can combine with a preceding vowel to produce diphthongs, e.g. *új* (pronounced $\overline{oo}$ʸ), *fej* (pronounced fæʸ), *sajt* (pronounced soyt). In all these cases, the **y** should be pronounced only fleetingly, as in boy.

Pronunciation of the Hungarian alphabet

A	o	**GY**	dʸe	**NY**	ænʸ	**T**	te
Á	aa	**H**	haa	**O**	aw	**TY**	tʸe
B	be*	**I**	ee	**Ó**	$\overline{aw}$	**U**	oo
C	tse	**Í**	$\overline{ee}$	**Ö**	ur	**Ú**	$\overline{oo}$
CS	tche	**J**	ye	**Ő**	$\overline{ur}$	**Ü**	ew
D	de	**K**	kaa	**P**	pe	**Ű**	$\overline{ew}$
E	æ	**L**	æl	**Q**	kew	**V**	ve
É	e	**LY**	ɔɔl eepseelon	**R**	ær	**W**	dooplovvay
F	ayf	**M**	æm	**S**	æsh	**Z**	ze
G	ghe	**N**	æn	**SZ**	æs	**ZS**	zhe

PRONUNCIATION

---

* e doesn't appear in the transcriptions, but has more or less the same value as **a** in late.

Some basic expressions

Yes.	**Igen.**	eegæn
No.	**Nem.**	næm
Please.	**Kérem.**	kayræm
Yes, please.	**Igen, kérem.**	eegæn kayræm
Thank you.	**Köszönöm.**	kursurnurm
No, thank you.	**Nem, köszönöm.**	næm kursurnurm
Thank you very much.	**Köszönöm szépen.**	kursurnurm saypæn
You're welcome.	**Szívesen.**	sēēvæshæn
Sorry.	**Sajnálom.**	shoynaalawm

Greetings

Good morning.	**Jó reggelt.**	yāw ræg-gælt
Good afternoon.	**Jó napot.**	yāw noppawt
Good evening.	**Jó estét.**	yāw æshtayt
Good night.	**Jó éjszakát.**	yāw ayᵞsokkaat
Goodbye.	**Viszontlátásra.**	veesawntlaataashro
See you later.	**Viszlát.**	veeslaat
This is Mr. ...	**Szeretném bemutatni... urat.**	sæerætnaym bæmoototnee ... oorot
This is Mrs. ...	**Szeretném bemutatni... urnőt.**	sæerætnaym bæmoototnee ... oornürt
This is Miss...	**Szeretném bemutatni... kisasszonyt.**	sæerætnaym bæmoototnee ... keeshoss-sawnᵞt
I'm pleased to meet you.	**Örülök, hogy megismerhetem.**	urrewlurk hawdᵞ mægeeshmærhætæm
How are you?	**Hogy van?**	hawdᵞ von
Very well, thank you. And you?	**Köszönöm, nagyon jól. És Ön?**	kursurnurm nodᵞawn yāwl. aysh urn

Questions

Where?	**Hol?**	hawl
Where is ...?	**Hol van ...?**	hawl von
Where are ...?	**Hol vannak ...?**	hawl **von**-nok
How?	**Hogy?**	hawd^y
How much?	**Mennyi/Mennyit?**	mæn^{y}ee/mæn^{y}eet
How many?	**Hány?**	haan^y
When?	**Mikor?**	meekawr
Why?	**Miért?**	meeayrt
Who?	**Ki?**	kee
Which?	**Melyik?**	mæ^{y}eek
What?	**Mi?**	mee
What do you call this/that?	**Mi a neve ennek/ annak?**	mee o nævæ æn-næk/ on-nok
What does this/ that mean?	**Ez/Az mit jelent?**	æz/oz meet yælænt

Do you speak ...?

Do you speak English/ French/German?	**Beszél angolul/ franciául/németül?**	bæsayl ongawlool/front-seeaaool/naymætewl
Does anyone here speak English?	**Van itt valaki aki angolul beszél?**	von eet vollokkee okkee ongawlool bæsayl
I don't speak much Hungarian.	**Alig beszélek magyarul.**	olleeg bæsaylæk mod^{y}o-rrool
How do you say this in Hungarian?	**Hogy mondják ezt magyarul?**	hawd^y mawnd^{y}aak æst mod^{y}orrool
I beg your pardon?	**Bocsánat de nem értem önt.**	bawchaanot dæ næm ayr-tæm urnt
Could you speak more slowly?	**Elmondaná lassabban?**	ælmawndonnaa losh-shob-bon
Could you repeat it?	**Megismételné?**	mægheeshmaytælnay

Please write it down.	**Kérem, írja ezt le.**	kayræm ēēryo æst læ
Can you translate this for me?	**Lefordítaná ezt nekem?**	læfawrdēētonnaa æst nækæm
Please point to the phrase in the book.	**Kérem, mutassa meg ezt a kifejezést a könyvben.**	kayræm mootosh-sho mæg æst o keefæyæzaysht o kurn^{V}vbæn
Just a minute. I'll see if I can find it in this book.	**Egy pillanat. Megnézem, benne van-e a könyvben.**	æd^V peel-lonnot. mægnayzæm bæn-næ von-æ o kurn^{V}vbæn
I understand.	**Értem.**	ayrtæm
I don't understand.	**Nem értem.**	næm ayrtæm
Do you understand?	**Ön érti?**	urn ayrtee

Can ...?

Can I have ...?	**Kaphatok ...?**	kophottawk
Can we have ...?	**Kaphatunk ...?**	kophottoonk
Can you show me ...?	**Megmutatná ...?**	mægmoototnaa
I can't.	**Nem tudok.**	næm toodawk
Can you tell me ...?	**Megmondaná ...?**	mægmawndonnaa
Can you help me, please?	**Segítene nekem?**	shæghēētænæ nækæm
Can you direct me to ...?	**Elvezetne a ...?**	ælvæzætnæ o

Wanting

I'd like ...	**Szeretnék ...**	sæærætnayk
We'd like ...	**Szeretnénk ...**	sæærætnaynk
Please give me ...	**Kérem, adjon ...**	kayræm od^{V}awn*
Please give me this/that.	**Kérem, adjon ezt/azt.**	kayræm od^{V}awn æst/ost
Please bring me ...	**Kérem, hozzon ...**	kayræm hawz-zawn

---

* j after **d** is pronounced like **gy** (d^V).

Please bring me this/that.	Hozzon kérem ezt/azt.	hawz-zawn kayræm æst/ost
I'm hungry.	Éhes vagyok.	ayhæsh vod^yawk
I'm thirsty.	Szomjas vagyok.	sawmyosh vod^yawk
I'm tired.	Fáradt vagyok.	faarot vod^yawk
I'm lost.	Eltévedtem.	æltayvædtæm
I'm looking for ...	A ...t keresem.	o...-t kæræshæm
It's important.	Fontos.	fawntawsh
It's urgent.	Sürgős.	shewrgūrsh
Hurry up!	Siessen!	sheeæsh-shæn

It is/There is ...

It is ...	Van ...	von
Is it ...?	Van ...?	von
It isn't ...	Nincs ...	neench
There is/There are ...	Van .../Vannak ...	von.../von-nok
Is there/Are there ...?	Van .../Vannak ...?	von.../von-nok
There isn't any.	Ez/Az nincs.	æz/oz neench
There aren't any.	Ezek/Azok nincsenek.	æzæk/ozzawk neenchænæk

A few common words

big/small	nagy/kicsi	nod^y/keechee
cheap/expensive	olcsó/drága	awlchaw/draago
good/bad	jó/rossz	yaw/rawss
better/worse	jobb/rosszabb	yawb/rawss-sob
right/wrong	helyes/helytelen	hæ^yæsh/hæ^ytælæn
easy/difficult	egyszerű/bonyolult	æd^ysærēw/bawn^yawloolt
light/heavy	könnyű/nehéz	kurn^yēw/næhayz
full/empty	teli/üres	tælee/ewræsh

free/occupied	**szabad/foglalt**	sobbod/fawglolt
open/shut	**nyitva/zárva**	n^{y}eetvo/zaarvo
old/young	**öreg/fiatal**	urræg/feeottol
old/new	**régi/új**	rayghee/$\overline{oo}^y$
quick/slow	**gyors/lassú**	d^{y}awrsh/losh-sh$\overline{oo}$
beautiful/ugly	**szép/csúnya**	sayp/ch$\overline{oo}$n^{y}o
warm/cold	**meleg/hideg**	mælæg/heedæg
never/always	**soha/mindig**	shawho/meendeeg
early/late	**korán/későn**	kawraan/kaysh$\overline{u}$rn
here/there	**itt/ott**	eet/awt
near/far	**közel/távol**	kurzæl/taavawl
left/right	**bal/jobb**	bol/yawb
first/last	**első/utolsó**	ælsh$\overline{u}$r/ootawlshaw
now/then	**ekkor/akkor**	æk-kawr/ok-kawr
immediately/later	**azonnal/később**	ozzawn-nol/kaysh$\overline{u}$rb

(side margin) SOME BASIC EXPRESSIONS

Some prepositions ...

at	**-kor** (time)	-kawr
	-nál/-nél (place)	-naal/-nayl
on	**-rá/-ra/-re/-on/**	-raa/-ro/-ræ/-awn
	-en/-ön	-æn/-urn
in	**-ban/-ben**	-bon/-bæn
before (time)	**előtt**	æl$\overline{u}$rt
before (place)	**előtt**	æl$\overline{u}$rt
after	**után**	ootaan
behind	**mögött**	murgurt
to	**felé/oda**	fælay/awdo
from	**-ból/-ből**	-b$\overline{aw}$l/-b$\overline{u}$rl
with	**-val/-vel**	-vol/-væl

---

* English prepositions are often rendered by suffixes in Hungarian. See p. 7.

without	**nélkül**	naylkewl
inside	**belül**	bælewl
outside	**kívül**	kēēvewl
through	**keresztül**	kæræstewl
towards	**felé**	fælay
up	**fent**	fænt
down	**lent**	lænt
above	**felett**	fælæt
below	**alatt**	ollot
over	**fölött**	furlurt
under	**alatt**	ollot
until	**eddig/addig**	æd-deeg/od-deeg
for	**-ért**	-ayrt
between	**között**	kurzurt
during	**közben**	kurzbæn
since	**óta**	āwto

... and a few more useful words

and	**és**	aysh
or	**vagy**	vod^y
but	**de**	dæ
not	**nem**	næm
nothing	**semmi**	sæm-mee
none	**egyik sem**	æd^{y}eek sæm
very	**nagyon**	nod^{y}awn
soon	**hamarosan**	hommorrawshon
perhaps	**talán**	tollaan
already	**már**	maar
again	**ismét**	eeshmayt
also	**is**	eesh

Arrival

You've arrived. Whether you come by train, plane, car or Danube steamer, you'll have to go through passport and customs formalities. (All except Austrian and Finnish nationals require a visa in addition to their passport.) If you didn't obtain one in advance through your travel agency or a Hungarian consulate, you can get one at road crossing points, river ports and at Budapest airport.

Customs officials and police on duty at crossing points speak some English and German.

Note: rail travellers *cannot* have a visa issued on the spot.

Passport control

Here's my passport.	**Tessék, az útlevelem.**	tæsh-shayk oz ōōtlævæ-læm
I'll be staying...	**...maradok.**	...morroddawk
a few days	**Néhány napig**	nayhaan^y noppeeg
a week	**Egy hétig**	æd^y hayteeg
2 weeks	**2 hétig**	2 hayteeg
a month	**Egy hónapig**	æd^y hāwnoppeeg
I don't know yet.	**Még nem tudom.**	mayg næm toodawm
I'm here on holiday.	**A szabadságomat töltöm itt.**	o sobbodshaagawmot turlturm eet
I'm here on business.	**Üzleti úton vagyok.**	ewzlætee ōōtawn vod^yawk
I'm just passing through.	**Csak átutazóban vagyok.**	chok aatootozzāwbon vod^yawk

If the going gets hard, say:

I'm sorry, I don't understand.	**Sajnálom, de nem értem.**	shoynaalawm dæ næm ayrtæm
Does anyone here speak English?	**Beszél itt valaki angolul?**	bæsayl eet vollokkee ongawlool

CAR/BORDER FORMALITIES: see page 146

Customs

After collecting your baggage, leave by the green exit if you have nothing to declare or by the red exit if you have goods on which you must pay duty. Spot checks are frequently made in the green channel.

The chart shows what main items you may take into Hungary duty-free.*

Cigarettes	Cigars	Tobacco	Spirits	Wine
250 or	40 or	200 g	1 l. and	2 l.

Narcotics and obscene publications will be confiscated, with more severe penalties reserved.

I've nothing to declare.	Nincs elvámolni valóm.	neench ælvaamawlnee vollāwm
I've a ...	Van egy ...	von æd^y
carton of cigarettes	karton cigarettám	kortawn tseegorræt-
bottle of whisky	üveg viszkim	taam ewvæg veeskeem
This is a gift.	Ez ajándék.	æz oyaandayk
It's for my personal use.	Ez a személyes használatomat szolgálja.	æz o sæmay^yæsh hosnaalottawmot sawlgaalyo
This is not new.	Ez nem új.	æz næm ōō^y

ARRIVAL

Kérem az útlevelét.	Your passport, please.
Önnek vízumra van szüksége. Legyen szíves jöjjön velem.	You need a visa. Come with me, please.
Kérem, nyissa ki ezt a táskát.	Please open this bag.
Ezért vámot kell fizetnie.	You'll have to pay duty on this.
Van még egyéb csomagja is?	Have you any more luggage?

* All allowances subject to change without notice.

Baggage – Porters

Porters are in short supply, though with perseverence you should be able to locate one. You'll generally find baggage trolleys. Against an extra tip, your taxi driver will help you.

Porter!	**Hordár!**	hawrdaar
Please take these bags.	**Kérem,vigye ezeket a bőröndöket.**	kayræm veed^Yæ æzækæt o būrrurndurkæt
That's my ...	**Ez az én ...**	æz oz ayn
bag/luggage suitcase	**táskám/csomagom bőröndöm**	taashkaam/chawmoggawm būrrurndurm
There's one piece missing.	**Egy csomag hiányzik.**	æd^Y chawmog heeaan^Y-zeek
Take these bags to the ...	**Kérem, vigye ezeket a csomagokat ...**	kayræm veed^Yæ æzækæt o chawmoggawkot
bus	**az autóbuszhoz**	oz oootāwbooss-hawz
taxi	**a taxihoz**	o toxeehawz
luggage lockers	**a csomagmegőrzőbe**	o chawmogmægūrrzūrbæ
Where are the baggage trolleys?	**Hol vannak a podgyász kézi-kocsik?**	hawl von-nok o pawd^Yaass kayzeekawcheek

Changing money

You'll find currency exchange facilities at the airport, major railway stations and all entry points for road traffic. If you arrive after hours, your hotel will be able to change a certain amount of dollars, pounds sterling or some other foreign currencies for you. Keep all receipts.

See page 134 for details of money and currency exchange as well as banking hours.

Where's the nearest currency exchange?	**Hol tudok valutát beváltani?**	hawl toodawk vollootaat bævaaltonnee
Can you change these traveller's cheques (checks)?	**Beváltják ezeket a traveller's csekkeket?**	bævaaltyaak æzækæt o trovvæl-lærs chæk-kækæt

TIPPING: see inside back cover

I want to change some ...	... akarok beváltani.	... okkorrawk bævaaltonnee
dollars	Dollárt	dawl-laart
pounds sterling	Angol fontot	ongawl fawntawt
Can you change this into forints?	Átváltaná ezt forintra?	aatvaaltonnaa æst fawreentro

Directions—Finding a room

Tourist information offices are to be found at Budapest international airport, major railway stations and border crossing points. They are often able to book you a hotel room if you arrive without a reservation. Some staff members may speak English or German.

How do I get to this address?	Hogy jutok el ide?	hawd^y yootawk æl eedæ
How do I get to this hotel?	Hogy jutok el ehhez a szállodához?	hawd^y yootawk æl æhhæz o saal-lawdaahawz
Is there a bus into town?	Van autóbuszjárat a városba?	von ooot$\overline{aw}$boosyaarot o vaarawshbo
Where can I get a taxi?	Hol kapok taxit?	hawl koppawk toxeet
Where can I hire a car?	Hol lehet autót bérelni?	hawl læhæt ooot$\overline{aw}$t bayrælnee
Have you a map of the town?	Van térképe a városról?	von tayrkaypæ o vaarawshr$\overline{aw}$l
Could you book me a hotel room, please?	Kérem, foglaljon részemre egy szobát.	kayræm fawglolyawn rayssæmræ æd^y sawbaat
in the town centre	a központban	o kurzpawntbon
near the station	az állomás mellett	oz aal-lawmaash mæl-læt
a single room	egy egyágyas szobát	æd^y æd^{y}aad^{y}osh sawbaat
a double room	egy kétágyas szobát	æd^y kaytaad^{y}osh sawbaat
not too expensive	nem túl drágát	næm t$\overline{oo}$l draagaat
Where is the hotel located?	Hol található a szálloda?	hawl tollaalhott$\overline{aw}$ o saal-lawdo

ARRIVAL

CHECKING IN: see page 30

Car rental

Car hire firms have offices at Budapest international airport and major railway stations. You can also hire a vehicle through a tourist office or your hotel. You must be at least twenty-one years of age and have held a full driving licence for more than one year. See the section beginning on page 142 for information on driving in Hungary.

You'll usually find someone at the agency who speaks English, but if not, use the following phrases to specify your requirements.

I'd like to hire a ... car.	**Egy ... kocsit szeretnék bérelni.**	æd^y ... **kaw**cheet **sæ**rætnayk **bayr**ælnee
large/small	**nagyot/kicsit**	nod^{y}awt/**kee**cheet
I'd like it for ...	**... szeretném.**	... **sæ**rætnaym
a day/4 days a week/2 weeks	**Egy napra/4 napra Egy hétre/2 hétre**	æd^y **no**pro/4 **no**pro æd^y **hay**træ/2 **hay**træ
What's the charge per ... ?	**Mennyi a bérleti díj ... ?**	**mæn**^{y}ee o **bayr**lætee dēē^y
day/week	**naponként/hetenként**	**nop**pawnkaynt/ **hæ**tænkaynt
Does that include mileage?	**A bérleti díjban a kilométer járulék is benne van?**	o **bayr**lætee dēē^{y}bon o **kee**lawmaytær **yaa**roolayk eesh bæn-næ von
What's the charge per kilometre?	**Mennyi a járulék kilométerenként?**	**mæn**^{y}ee o **yaa**roolayk **kee**lawmaytærænkaynt
Is petrol (gas) included?	**Ebben benn van az üzemanyag költsége?**	æb-bæn bæn von oz **ew**zæmon^{y}og **kurl**tshaygæ
I want full insurance.	**Casco biztosítást kérek.**	**kosh**kaw **beez**tawshēētaasht **kay**ræk
I'll be doing about 200 kilometres.	**Körülbelül 200 kilométert utazom a kocsival.**	**kur**rewbælewl 200 **kee**lawmaytært **oo**tozzawm o **kaw**cheevol
What's the deposit?	**Mennyi a garanciális letét?**	**mæn**^{y}ee o **gor**rontseeaaleesh **læ**tayt
I've a credit card.	**Rendelkezem hitelkártyával.**	**ræn**dælkæzæm **hee**tælkaart^{y}aavol

SIGHTSEEING: see page 75

ARRIVAL

Taxi

All taxis have meters. When they are free, the rooftop *Taxi* sign is lit. (Avoid private cars which might offer you taxi services—they are illegal, and you would face problems in case of accident.) It's advisable to state your destination before entering the cab, as a driver may refuse trips which are too long or out of the way.

If your journey takes you beyond the city limits, you will be charged the return fare up to the city limits. It's customary to give a tip in addition to the amount shown on the meter.

Where can I get a taxi?	**Hol kapok taxit?**	hawl **koppawk** toxeet
Please get me a taxi.	**Kérem, szerezzen egy taxit.**	kayræm særæz-zæn æd^y toxeet
What's the fare to …?	**… -ig mennyi a viteldíj?**	…-eeg mæn^yee o veetæl-dee^y
Take me to …	**Kérem, vigyen el …**	kayræm veed^yæn æl
this address	**erre a címre**	ær-ræ o tseemræ
the airport	**a repülőtérre**	o ræpewlūrtayr-ræ
the station	**a vasútállomásra**	o voshōōtaal-lawmaashro
the … Hotel	**a … szállóba**	o … saal-lāwbo
the city centre	**a városközpontba**	o vaarawshkurzpawntbo
Turn … at the next corner.	**Forduljon … a következő sarkon.**	fawrdoolyawn… o kurvætkæzūr shorkawn
left	**balra**	bolro
right	**jobbra**	yawbro
Stop here, please.	**Kérem, itt álljon meg.**	kayræm eet aalyawn mæg
I'm in a hurry.	**Sietek.**	sheeætæk
Could you drive more slowly, please?	**Kérem, hajtson lassabban.**	kayræm hoytshawn losh-shob-bon
Would you help me carry my bags?	**Kérem, segítsen vinni a podgyászt.**	kayræm shægheetshæn veennee o pawd^yaast
Would you please wait for me?	**Kérem, várjon.**	kayræm vaaryawn

ARRIVAL

TIPPING: see inside back-cover

Hotel—Other accommodation

Hotel rooms are often in short supply, both in the capital and in popular tourist areas such as around Lake Balaton. Whenever possible, make your bookings well in advance though your home travel agency, and take along written confirmation so as to avoid any misunderstandings on the spot. The busiest periods are the summer holiday season and any time when trade fairs, exhibitions or major international conferences are being held, particularly in Budapest. Travel agencies in your own country will probably be able to give you the precise dates of such events. Otherwise you may like to write to one of the foreign agencies of *Ibusz*, the Hungarian national tourist organization. They are located in the following cities in western Europe: Brussels, Cologne, Frankfurt, London, Paris, Rome, Stockholm and Vienna. There is also an *Ibusz* office in New York. Your home travel agency will be able to give your their addresses.

Students might ask their national student travel service for details of inexpensive accommodation available in Hungary. You should take along an international student identity card if you intend to make use of such facilities.

Should you arrive in the country without prearranged accommodation, there are several offices you can turn to for assistance in finding a room. Tourist information offices are maintained at virtually all entry points. Local travel agencies may also make reservations for you. If hotels are full, they may be able to put you up in private homes. A booking fee is charged for on-the-spot reservations.

Rates are up to 30 per cent lower outside the main summer tourist season. A room for two works out appreciably cheaper than two single rooms.

CAMPING: see page 90

Szálloda
(saal-lawdo)

Hotels large and small go under this name (though the foreign word "hotel" is also used quite widely). They are graded by stars, from 5-star de-luxe establishments to 1-star budget hotels.

Only two or three top-rank international hotels in the capital are air-conditioned. Very few have swimming pools or saunas. Hotels are clean and standards of service acceptable, depending on the category of hotel. Most 3-, 4- and 5-star hotels offer shopping arcades, tourist and airline offices and a variety of sightseeing programs.

Motel
(mawtæl)

These are relatively rare in Hungary. Most are to be found along the shores of Lake Balaton as well as at some principal road junctions.

Fizetővendég-szolgálat
(feezætūrvæn-daygsawlgaalot)

This is the term for private accommodation, a service operated by most travel agencies both in Budapest and throughout the country. In Budapest, rates overlap with those of modest hotels, but in the countryside they are usually very moderate. You may have the choice of room only or with breakfast included. Bathroom facilities, generally shared, are available.

Along major roads and in holiday centres you will also see numerous signs for private accommodation reading *Szoba kiadó* or, in German, *Fremdenzimmer*. Both are the equivalent of the English "Bed and Breakfast". Feel free to knock on the door yourself, phrase book in hand—there's no need to go through an agency for this type of accommodation.

HOTEL

Checking in—Reception

My name is ...	... vagyok.	... vod^yawk
I've a reservation.	**Már foglaltam szobát.**	maar fawgloltom sawbaat
We've reserved two rooms, one single and a double.	**Két szobát foglaltunk, egy egyágyasat és egy kétágyasat.**	kayt sawbaat fawgloltoonk æd^y æd^yaad^yoshot aysh æd^y kaytaad^yoshot
Here's the confirmation.	**Itt a visszaigazolásuk.**	eet o vess-so-eegozzawlaashook
I'd like a ...	**Szeretnék ...**	særætnayk
single room	**egyágyas szobát**	æd^yaad^yosh sawbaat
double room	**kétágyas szobát**	kaytaad^yosh sawbaat
room with a bath	**fürdőszobás szobát**	fewrdūrsawbaash sawbaat
room with a shower	**egy szobát zuhannyal**	æd^y sawbaat zoohan^yol
room with a balcony	**erkélyes szobát**	ærkay^yæsh sawbaat
room with a view	**szobát szép kilátással**	sawbaat sayp keelaataash-shol
in the front	**az utcai oldalon**	oz oottsoee awldollawn
at the back	**a hátsó oldalon**	o haatshāw awldollawn
facing the lake	**amelyik a tóra néz**	ommæ^yeek o tāwro nayz
facing the courtyard	**az udvari oldalon**	oz oodvorree awldollawn
It must be quiet.	**Egy csendes szobát kérek.**	æd^y chændæsh sawbaat kayræk
I'd like a room a bit higher up/lower down.	**A szobát egy kissé feljebb/lejjebb szeretném.**	o sawbaat æd^y keesh-shay fælyæb/læ^y-yæb særætnaym
Is there ...?	**Van ...?**	von
central heating	**központifűtés**	kurzpawnteefēwtaysh
a radio in the room	**rádió a szobában**	raadeeāw o sawbaabon
a TV set in the room	**TV a szobában**	tayvay o sawbaabon
room service	**felszolgálás a szobában**	fælsawlgaalaash o sawbaabon
hot water	**meleg víz**	mælæg vēēz
running water	**hideg víz**	heedæg vēēz
a private toilet	**külön W.C.**	kewlurn vaytsay

In the higher-category hotels, most of the staff at the reception desk speak some English or German.

How long?

We'll be staying ...	... maradunk.	... morroddoonk
overnight only	Csak erre az éjszakára	chock ær-ræ oz ay^yssokkaaro
a few days	Néhány napig	nayhaan^y noppeeg
a week (at least)	(Legalább) egy hétig	(lægollaab) æd^y hayteeg
I don't know yet.	Még nem tudom.	mayg næm toodawm

How much?

What's the price ...?	Mennyibe kerül ...?	mæn^yeebæ kærewl
per night	egy éjszakára	æd^y ay^yssokkaaro
per week	egy hétre	æd^y haytræ
for bed and breakfast	a szoba reggelivel	o sawbo ræg-gæleevæl
without meals	étkezés nélkül	aytkæzaysh naylkewl
for half board	napi két étkezéssel	noppee kayt aytkæzayshshayl
Does that include ...?	Ez magában foglalja ...?	æz moggaabon fawglolyo
service	a kiszolgálási díjat	o keessawlgaalaashee deeyot
resort tax	az üdülőhelyi illetéket	oz ewdewlurhæ^yee eel-lætaykæt
Is there any reduction for children?	Van kedvezmény a gyerekek után?	von kædvæzmayn^y o d^yærækæk ootaan

Decision

May I see the room?	Megnézhetem a szobát?	mægnayzhætæm o sawbaat
I asked for a room with a bath.	Egy fürdőszobás szobát rendeltem.	æd^y fewrdursawbaash sawbaat rændæltæm
Do you have anything ...?	Volna egy ... szobájuk?	vawlno æd^y ... sawbaayook
better/bigger	jobb/nagyobb	yawb/nod^yawb
cheaper/quieter	olcsóbb/csendesebb	awlchawb/chændæshæb
That's fine. I'll take it.	Ez jó lesz. Ezt kiveszem.	æz yaw læs. æst keevæsæm

NUMBERS: see page 175

HOTEL

Registration

Upon arrival at a hotel, motel or private boarding house, you'll have to fill in a registration form *(bejelentőlap)*. If it doesn't carry an English translation, ask:

What does this mean?	**Ez mit jelent?**	æz meet yælænt

If you don't understand what he's saying, show him this section:

Megkaphatom az útlevelét?	May I see your passport, please?
Legyen szíves, töltse ki ezt a bejelentőlapot.	Would you mind filling in this registration form?
Kérem, itt írja alá.	Please sign here.
Meddig marad?	How long will you be staying?

What's my room number?	**Mi a szoba számom?**	mee o sawbo saamawm
Where can I park my car?	**Hol hagyhatom a kocsimat?**	hawl hod^yhottawm o kawcheemot
I'd like to leave this in your safe.	**Ezt a széfjükben szeretném hagyni.**	æzt o sayfyewkbæn særætnaym hod^ynee
Will you have my luggage sent up?	**Felvitetné a csomagjaimat?**	fælveetætnay o chawmod^yoeemot
Will you please wake me up at …?	**Kérem ébresszen fel … órakor.**	kayræm aybræs-sæn fæl… āwrokawr

The bill (check)

Bills are usually paid weekly or, of course, upon departure if you stay less than a week. A 10-15 per cent service charge is generally included in the bill, but you may like to ask:

Is service included?	**A felszolgálási díj benne van az árban?**	o fælsawlgaalaashee dee^y bæn-næ von oz aarbon

Tipping is practically a must in Hungary. See inside back cover.

TELLING THE TIME: see page 178

Service, please!

Now that you are safely installed, meet some members of the hotel staff:

bellboy	kifutó	keefootāw
maid	szobalány	sawbollaan^y
manager	szálloda igazgató	saal-lawdo eegozgottāw
porter	hordár	hawrdaar
switchboard operator	telefonközpontos	tælæfawnkurzpawntawsh
waiter	pincér	peentsayr
waitress	pincérnő	peentsayrnūr

If you want to address members of the staff, you don't use the actual names shown above, but a general introductory phrase:

Excuse me …	Elnézést …	ælnayzaysht

General requirements

Please ask the maid to come up.	Kérem, küldje fel a szobalányt.	kayræm kewld^yæ fæl o sawbollaan^yt
Who is it?	Ki az?	kee oz
Just a minute.	Egy pillanat.	æd^y peel-lonnot
Come in!	Jöjjön be!	yur^y-yurn bæ
Please bring us …	Kérem, hozzon nekünk …	kayræm hawz-zawn nækewnk
2 cups of coffee	2 csésze kávét	2 chayssæ kaavayt
a sandwich	egy szendvicset	æd^y sændveechæt
Can we have breakfast in our room?	Reggelizhetünk a szobában?	ræg-gæleez-hætewnk o sawbaabon
What's the voltage here?	Milyen a feszültség?	mee^yæn o fæsewltshayg
Is there a bath on this floor?	Van fürdőszoba ezen az emeleten?	von fewrdūrsawbo æzæn oz æmælætæn
Can you get me a babysitter?	Tudnának egy bébiszittert szerezni?	toodnaanok æd^y baybeesseet-tært særæznee

May I have a/an/some ...?	**Kaphatok ...?**	kophottawk
ashtray	**egy hamutálcát**	æd^y hommooltaaltsaat
bath towel	**egy fürdőtörülközőt**	æd^y fewrdürturrewlkurzürt
extra blanket	**egy plusz takarót**	æd^y plooss tokkorrawt
envelopes	**egy borítékot**	æd^y bawreetaykawt
(more) hangers	**vállfákat**	vaalfaakot
hot-water bottle	**ágymelegítőt**	aad^{y}mælægheetürt
ice cubes	**jégkockákat**	yaygkawtskaakot
needle and thread	**tűt, cérnát**	tēwt tsayrnaat
reading lamp	**egy olvasólámpát**	æd^y awlvoshawlaampaat
soap	**szappant**	sop-pont
writing paper	**levélpapírt**	lævaylpoppēert
Where's the ...?	**Hol van ...?**	hawl von
bathroom	**a fürdőszoba**	o fewrdürsawbo
cocktail lounge	**a koktél bár**	o kawktayl baar
dining room	**az étterem**	oz ayt-tæræm
emergency exit	**a vészkijárat**	o vayskee^{y}aarot
hairdresser's	**a fodrász**	o fawdraass
telephone	**a telefon**	o tælæfawn
television room	**a TV szoba**	o tayvay sawbo
toilet	**a W.C.**	o vaytsay

Breakfast

The Hungarian breakfast is a very substantial affair and is considered one of the most important meals of the day. It may consist of rolls and butter, jam, salami, cheese and eggs. Some even like a dish of excellent goulash or some stew to start off the day. If this is too much for you, just specify what you would like from the following list.

I'd like breakfast, please.	**Reggelizni szeretnék.**	ræg-gæleeznee særætnayk
I'll have some ...	**Kérek ...**	kayræk
cocoa	**kakaót**	kokkoawt
coffee	**kávét**	kaavayt
with whipped cream	**tejszínhabbal**	tæ^{y}sseenhob-bol
with milk	**tejjel**	tæ^y-yæl
juice	**gyümölcslét**	d^{y}ewmurlchlayt
grapefruit	**grépfrutot**	graypfrootawt
orange	**narancslét**	norronchlayt

EATING OUT: see page 38

milk	tejet	tæ^yæt
hot	melegen	mælægæn
cold	hidegen	heedægæn
tea	egy teát	æd^y tayaat
with milk	tejjel	tæ^y-yæl
with lemon	citrommal	tseetrawm-mol
May I have a/some …?	**Kaphatok …?**	kophottawk
boiled egg	főtt tojást	fūrt taw^yaasht
hard	kemény tojást	kæmayn^y taw^yaasht
medium	közepes tojást	kurzæpæsh taw^yaasht
soft	lágy tojást	laad^y taw^yaasht
bread	kenyeret	kæn^yæræt
butter	vajat	voyot
cheese	egy adag sajtot	æd^y oddog shoytawt
crescent rolls	kiflit	keefleet
fried eggs	tükör tojást	tewkurr taw^yaasht
ham and eggs	sonkát tojással	shawnkaat taw^yaash-shol
honey	mézet	mayzæt
jam	egy adag lekvárt	æd^y oddog lækvaart
rolls	péksüteményt	paykshewtæmayn^yt
salami	egy adag szalámit	æd^y oddog sollaameet
scrambled eggs	tojásrántottát	taw^yaashraantawt-taat
toast	egy adag tésztát	æd^y oddog taystaat
yoghurt	egy joghurtot	æd^y yawghoortawt
Would you bring me some …?	**Kérem, hozzon nekem …?**	kayræm hawz-zawn nækæm
cream	tejszínt	tæ^ysseent
lemon	citromot	tseetrawmawt
pepper	borsot	bawrshawt
salt	sót	shāwt
sugar	cukrot	tsookrawt
(a glass of) water	(egy pohár) vizet	(æd^y pawhaar) veezæt
hot water	forróvizet	fawr-rāwveezæt

Difficulties

But perhaps there's something wrong…

The … doesn't work.	A … nem működik.	o … næm mēwkurdeek
heating	fűtés	fēwtaysh
light	világítás	veelaaghēētaash
radiator	fűtőtest	fēwtūrtæsht
radio	rádió	raadeeāw

shower	**zuhany**	zoohon^y
tap	**csap**	chop
television	**TV**	tayvay
toilet	**W.C.**	vaytsay
ventilator	**ventillátor**	vænteel-laatawr

The washbasin is clogged.	**A mosdó el van dugulva.**	o mawshdaw æl von doogoolvo
The window is jammed.	**Az ablak be van szorulva.**	oz oblok bæ von sawroolvo
The blind is stuck.	**A roló fennakadt.**	o rawlaw fænokkodt
These aren't my shoes.	**Ez nem az én cipőm.**	æz næm oz ayn tseepurm
This isn't my laundry.	**Ez nem az én fehérnemüm.**	æz næm oz ayn fæhayrnæmewm
There's no hot water.	**Nincs melegvíz.**	neench mælægveez
My room has not been made up.	**Nem rakták rendbe a szobámat.**	næm roktaak rændbæ o sawbaamot
I've left the key in my room.	**A szobában felejtettem a kulcsomat.**	o sawboabon fælæy-tættæm o koolchawmot
The bulb is burnt out.	**Kiégett a körte.**	keeaygæt o kurrtæ
The ... is broken.	**Eltörött ...**	ælturrurt
lamp	**a lámpa**	o laampo
plug	**a dugasz**	o doogoss
shutter	**a zsalu**	o zholloo
socket	**a konektor**	o kawnæktawr
switch	**a kapcsoló**	o kopchawlaw
venetian blind	**a redőny**	o rædurn^y
window shade	**az ablakroló**	oz oblokrawlaw
Can you get it repaired?	**Meg tudja javíttatni?**	mæg toodyo yovveetotnee

Telephone—Mail—Callers

Can you get me London 123 4567?	**Kérem, hívja fel a London 123 4567 számot!**	kayræm heevyo fæl o lawndawn 123 4567 saamawt
Has anyone phoned for me?	**Keresett valaki?**	kæræshæt vollokkee

POST OFFICE AND TELEPHONE: see pages 137–141

HOTEL SERVICE

Is there any mail for me?	Van a részemre posta?	von o rayssæmræ pawshto
Are there any messages for me?	Érkezett a részemre valami üzenet?	ayrkæzæt o rayssæmræ vollommee ewzænæt
Do you sell stamps?	Postabélyegük van?	pawshtobbay^Vægewk von
Would you please post this for me?	Kérem, feladná ezt nekem?	kayræm fælodnaa æst nækæm

Checking out

May I have my bill?	Kérem, a számlámat.	kayræm o saamlaamot
I must leave at once.	Rögtön indulnom kell.	rurgturn eendoolnawm kæl
We'll be checking out soon/around noon.	Korán elutazunk./ Dél körül utazunk el.	kawraan ælootozzoonk/ dayl kurrewl ootozzoonk æl
I'm leaving early tomorrow. Please have my bill ready.	Holnap korán utazom el. Kérem, készítsék el a számlámat.	hawlnop kawraan ootozzawm æl. kayræm kayssēētshayk æl o saamlaamot
Is everything included?	Ebben minden szerepel?	æb-bæn meendæn særæpæl
You've made a mistake in this bill, I think.	Azt hiszem, hibásan állította össze a számlát.	ost heessæm heebaashon aal-lēētawt-to urs-sæ o saamlaat
When's the next ... to Vienna?	Mikor indul a következő ... Bécsbe?	meekawr eendool o kurvætkæzūr ... baychbæ
bus/plane/train	autóbusz/repülő/ vonat	ooootāwbooss/ræpewlūr/ vawnot
Would you get me a taxi?	Hívna egy taxit?	hēēvno æd^y toxeet
Would you please have somebody bring down our luggage?	Kérem, küldjön valakit, aki leviszi a csomagjainkat.	kayræm kewld^Vurn vollokkeet okkee læveessee o chawmogyo-eenkot
We're in a great hurry.	Borzasztóan sietünk.	bawrzostāwon sheeætewnk
Here's my forwarding address.	Ez a következő címem.	æz o kurvætkæzūr tsēēmæm
It's been a very enjoyable stay.	Nagyon jól éreztük itt magunkat.	nod^Vawn yāwl ayræztewk eet moggoonkot

TAXI: see page 27

HOTEL SERVICE

Eating out

There are many different types of places in which to enjoy meals and drink, from simple snackbars to luxury restaurants:

Bisztró
(beestrāw)

A small restaurant, generally offering reasonably priced standard meals and drinks, including coffee and tea, at any time during opening hours. Usually frequented by people in a hurry.

Büfé
(bewfay)

Found at railway and bus stations, in shopping centres and department stores, buffets serve hot and cold sandwiches, cakes, desserts and all kind of drinks including coffee and tea. Some are open round the clock. Prices are reasonable.

Csárda
(chaardo)

A country inn, usually offering regional food and drink specialities in the medium price range. In the evening, gypsy bands often provide romantic music to go with the meal. Found mainly on major highways.

Cukrászda
(tsookraazdo)

A pastry shop serving sandwiches, cakes, desserts, ice cream, soft drinks, coffee, tea and alcoholic drinks. Larger establishments have light or pop music, either taped or live. Prices tend to be rather high.

Étkező
(aytkæzǖr)

A small inn, often with only a few tables, serving regional specialities, local wines and beer at modest prices.

Étterem
(ayt-tæræm)

The traditional restaurant, serving a wide range of dishes and drinks. These establishments are classified according to location, facilities and standard of service, with the category indicated on the menu (see page 40). Prices do not necessarily reflect quality of food, and the self-same dish may cost much more in a first-class restaurant than in a modest one. Gypsy bands often play at night. In a hotel *étterem*, price and quality depend on the category of the hotel.

Kifőzés (keefűrzaysh)	A small, low-priced inn, often a family concern, open mainly during the tourist season. First-class country food as well as local wine and beer are served. In the Lake Balaton area some of these establishments are famous for their gourmet creations.
Önkiszolgáló (urnkeessawlgaalāw)	A self-service snackbar-type establishment. Mostly located in town centres and near railway stations, they are inexpensive but not always too clean.
Snackbár ("snackbar")	A superior *önkiszolgáló* offering sandwiches, cakes and all kinds of drinks including espresso coffee and tea at slightly higher prices.
Vendéglő (vændayglūr)	A larger restaurant, usually with rustic décor, serving moderately priced meals and all kinds of drinks. Good gypsy music is often played at night.

Mainly for drinking

Borozó (bawrawzāw)	A wine bar, offering a variety of wines and some snacks. Prices vary widely.
Borpince (bawrpeentsæ)	A wine cellar, usually run by a wine-producing cooperative or farm. Exceptionally high-quality wines and light food are available at moderate prices.
Drinkbár ("drinkbar")	A bar, frequented mostly by tourists, serving mainly spirits (liquor). Prices are high.
Eszpresszó (æspræss-sāw)	A small coffee bar offering mainly espresso coffee but also some other non-alcoholic and alcoholic beverages at moderate prices. Light refreshments and ice-cream are also available.
Mulató (moolottāw)	A modest nightclub, with a minor floor show. The accent is on expensive imported spirits. Light snacks are available.
Söröző (surrurzūr)	A beer hall, with moderate prices. Some imported beers are available but at higher prices.
Tejbár/Tejivó (tæ^ybaar/tæ^yeevāw)	Milkbars go under either of these two names. In addition to milk and milk-based drinks, sandwiches, cakes and other snacks are available, all at very reasonable prices. Just the place for breakfast or a mid-morning snack.

Meals and menus

By law, all eating places must offer at least two complete set menus (*napi menü*—**no**ppee **mæ**new) at low to moderate prices. These menus typically comprise a soup, a main course and dessert or fruit. However, many people prefer to order à la carte. As a rule, drinks are listed on a separate card and they may be served by a different waiter. Some top restaurants also offer special dishes for those on certain diets as well as smaller portions for children. It is customary to tip the waiter 8–10 per cent of the bill, depending on quality of service.

You will generally see one or more of the following explanatory notices on the bill of fare:

I. osztályu étterem	First-class restaurant
II. osztályu étterem	Second-class restaurant
III. osztályu étterem	Third-class restaurant
Osztályon felüli étterem.	Top-class restaurant
Az árak köret nélkül értendők.	Prices do not include garnishes.
Az ételeket körettel szolgáljuk fel.	Meals are served with garnishes.
Az X—el jelölt ételek elfogytak.	Meals marked with X are no longer available.
... Ft. kötelező fogyasztás.	Minimum order: ... forints.

Meal times

Breakfast (*reggeli*—**ræg**-gælee): 7–10 a.m.

Lunch (*ebéd*—**æ**bayd): noon–2 or 3 p.m.

Dinner (*vacsora*—**vo**chawro): 7–10 or 11 p.m.

Restaurants in leading hotels will often serve à-la-carte meals in your room round the clock.

BREAKFAST: see page 34

Hungry

I'm hungry/I'm thirsty.	Éhes vagyok/ Szomjas vagyok.	ayhæsh vod^Yawk/ sawmyosh vod^Yawk
Can you recommend a good restaurant?	Ajánlana egy jó éttermet?	oyaanlonno æd^Y yā̄w ayt-tærmæt
Are there any inexpensive restaurants around here?	Találhatók a környéken olcsó éttermek?	tollaalhottā̄wk o kurr- n^Yaykæn awlchā̄w ayt- tærmæk

To be sure of getting a table in a well-known restaurant it's advisable to reserve your table in advance by telephone.

I'd like to book a table for 4, please.	4 fő részére szeretnék asztalt foglalni.	4 fū̄r rayssayræ særæt- nayk ostolt fawglolnee
We'll come at 8.	8 órakor jövünk.	8 ā̄wrokkawr yurvewnk

EATING OUT

Asking and ordering

Good evening. I'd like a table for 2.	Jó estét kívánok. 2 fő részére kérek egy asztalt.	yā̄w æshtayt keevaanawk. 2 fū̄r rayssayræ kayræk æd^Y ostolt
I've reserved a table for 4.	4 fő részére rendeltem asztalt.	4 fū̄r rayssayræ rændæltæm ostolt
Could we have a table ...?	Lenne szabad asztaluk ...?	læn-næ sobbod ostollook
in the corner	a sarokban	o shorrawkbon
by the window	az ablaknál	oz obloknaal
outside	kinnt	keent
on the terrace	a teraszon	o tærossawn
Are these seats taken?	Ezek a helyek foglaltak?	æzæk o hæ^Yæk fawgloltok
Waiter!/Waitress!	Pincér!/Pincérnő!	peentsayr/peentsayrnū̄r
I'd/We'd like something to drink/ eat.	Szeretnék/Szeret- nénk valamit inni/ enni.	særætnayk/særætnaynk vollommeet een-nee/ æn-nee
What are the set menus?	Mi a mai menü?	mee o moee mænew

NUMBERS: see page 175

May I have the menu and the drinks card?	Kérem az étlapot és az itallapot.	kayræm oz aytloppawt aysh oz eetol-loppawt
Can you serve me straight away? I'm in a hurry.	Azonnali kiszolgálást kérek. Sietek.	ozzawn-nollee keessawlgaalaasht kayræk. sheeætæk
Could we have a plate for the child, please?	Hozna egy tányért a gyereknek?	hawzno æd^y taan^yayrt o d^yæræknæk
Do you have any local dishes?	Ajánlana valami helyi különlegességet?	oyaanlonno vollommee hæ^yee kewlurnlægæsh-shaygæt
What's this?	Ez mi?	æz mee
Could we have a/an/ some ..., please?	Kaphatunk ...?	kophottoonk

another chair	még egy széket	mayg æd^y saykæt
ashtray	egy hamutartót	æd^y hommootortāwt
bottle of ...	egy üveg ...-t*	æd^y ewvæg ...-t
fork	egy villát	æd^y veel-laat
glass	egy poharat	æd^y pawhorrot
glass of water	egy pohár vizet	æd^y pawhaar veezæt
knife	egy kést	æd^y kaysht
lighter	egy öngyújtót	æd^y urnd^yōō^ytāwt
matches	gyufát	d^yoofaat
plate	egy tányért	æd^y taan^yayrt
serviette	egy szalvétát	æd^y solvaytaat
spoon	egy kanalat	æd^y konnollot
toothpicks	fogpiszkálót	fawgpeeskaalāwt

Mit parancsol?	What would you like?
Szabad ezt ajánlanom?	May I recommend this?
Mit óhajt inni?	What would you like to drink?
Sajnos, nem szolgálhatunk ... val.	We don't have any ...
Parancsol ...-t?	Do you want ...?

---

* See Grammar section for word endings.

I'd like ...	Kérnék ...	kayrnayk
aperitif	egy aperitívet	æd^Y opæreetēēvæt
appetizer	elöételt	æluraytælt
beer	sört	shurrt
bread	kenyeret	kæn^{Y}æræt
butter	vajat	voyot
cheese	sajtot	shoytawt
chicken	csirkét	cheerkayt
chips (Br.)	sült burgonyát	shewlt boorgawn^{Y}aat
coffee	kávét	kaavayt
dessert	édességet	aydæsh-shaygæt
fish	halat	hollot
French fries	sült burgonyát	sewlt boorgawn^{Y}aat
fruit	gyümölcsöt	d^{Y}ewmurlchurt
fruit juice	gyümölcslét	d^{Y}ewmurlchlayt
game	vadas ételt	voddosh aytælt
goulash	gulyáslevest	goo^{Y}aashlævæsht
ice-cream	fagylaltot	fod^{Y}loltawt
ketchup	ketchupot	kæchurpurt
lemonade	limonádét	leemawnaadayt
lettuce	fejes-salátát	fæ^{Y}aysh shollaataat
meat	húst	hōōsht
milk	tejet	tæ^{Y}æt
mineral water	ásványvizet	aashvaan^{Y}veezæt
mustard	mustárt	mooshtaart
noodles	metéltet	mætayltæt
oil	étolajat	aytawloyot
pepper	borsot	bawrshawt
potatoes	burgonyát	boorgawn^{Y}aat
poultry	szárnyast	saarn^{Y}osht
rice	rizst	reezht
rolls	péksüteményt	paykshewtæmayn^{Y}t
saccharine	szaharint	sohorreent
salad	salátát	shollaataat
salt	sót	shāwt
sandwich	szendvicset	sændveechæt
soft drink	üditőitalt	ewdeetūr-eetolt
soup	levest	lævæsht
spaghetti	spagettit	shpoggæt-teet
sugar	cukrot	tsookrawt
tea	teát	tæaat
vegetables	főzeléket	fūrzælaykæt
vinegar	ecetet	ætsætæt
water	vizet	veezæt
wine	bort	bawrt

EATING OUT

What's on the menu?

Our menu is presented according to courses. Under each heading you'll find an alphabetical list of dishes likely to be offered on a Hungarian menu, with their English equivalents. You can also show the book to the waiter. Should you want some soup, for example, show him the corresponding list and let him point to what's available. Use pages 41-44 for ordering in general.

In Hungary, a typical à-la-carte meal consists of soup, an entrée, the main course and then a dessert or cheese. Many enjoy an aperitif to start off with and accompany the meal with one or two matching wines. (If you prefer beer or mineral water, your choice will raise no eyebrows.) Invariably, the occasion is rounded off with a good, strong coffee and a fruit brandy.

Here, then, is our guide to good eating and drinking. Just turn to the section you want.

Appetizers

Restaurants offer a rich choice of both international and typically Hungarian appetizers, both hot and cold. For a light meal it's quite acceptable to take a soup, then an appetizer, and skip the rest.

I'd like a ...	... is kérnék.	... eesh **kayr**nayk
cold appetizer	**Hideg előételek**	**hee**dæg ælū̄raytælæk
hot appetizer	**Meleg előételek**	**mæ**læg ælū̄raytælæk
What would you recommend?	**Mit ajánlana?**	meet oyaanlonno

Cold appetizers

apró fánk	op**rāw** faank	small chicken fritter
bécsi hering-saláta	**bay**chee **hæ**reeng-shollaato	herring salad Vienna style (with vinegar)
dinnye koktél	**deen**Yæ **kawk**tayl	melon cocktail
dinnye sonkával	**deen**Yæ **shawn**kaavol	melon with ham
francia saláta	**front**seeo **sho**llaato	Russian salad
halmajonéz	**hol**moyawnayz	fish with mayonnaise
jérce koktél	**yayrt**sæ **kawk**tayl	chicken cocktail
kaszinó tojás	**ko**sseenāw **taw**Yaash	eggs with mayonnaise
kaviár	**ko**vveeaar	caviar
majonézes kukorica	**mo**yawnayzæsh **koo**kawreetso	sweetcorn with mayonnaise
orosz hússaláta	**aw**rawss **hōō**sh-shollaato	Russian salad with meat
ráksaláta	**raak**shollaato	crab salad
töltött tojás kaviárral	**tur**lturt **taw**Yaash **ko**vvoeaar-rol	eggs stuffed with caviar
alföldi saláta (**ol**furldee **sho**llaato)		salad Alföldi style ("Puszta salad"): slices of sausage in a vinaigrette sauce (oil, vinegar, herbs)
almás cékla (**ol**maash **tsay**klo)		apple slices and diced beetroot in a vinaigrette sauce
fokhagymás majonézes fejes saláta (**fawk**hodYmaash **mo**yawnayzæsh fæYæsh **sho**llaato)		lettuce salad with garlic-flavoured mayonnaise

hortobágyi húsos palacsinta
(**hawr**tawbaad^Yee **hōō**shawsh pollocheento)

stuffed omelet Hortobágy style: filled with veal or pork meat and sour cream, then briefly gratinated

libamáj pastétom
(**lee**bommaa^Y **paash**taytawm)

goose-liver paté mixed with butter and béchamel (white) sauce, spices and brandy, served in a flaky-pastry shell

omlet debreceni módra
(**awm**læt **dæb**rætsænee **mā̄w**dro)

omelet Debrecen stype: filled with *lecsó* (a mix of sliced green peppers, tomatoes, rice ans spices) and dry sausage slices

veseszeletek paradicsommal
(**væsh**æsælætæk **por**roddeechawm-mol)

kidney slices with tomato

Hot appetizers

csirág csőben sütve
cheeraag ch**ū̄r**bæn shewtvæ
baked asparagus

libamáj rizottó
lee**bom**aa^Y reezawt-tā̄w
goose-liver risotto

tálon sült tojás
taalawn shewlt taw^Yaash
fried eggs, meat slices

zöldbab csőben sütve
zurldbob ch**ū̄r**bæn shewtvæ
and vegetables fried string beans

gombafejek májkrémmel töltve
(**gawm**boffæ^Yæk maa^Ykraymmæl turltvæ)

mushrooms stuffed with liver paté

halsaláta szegedi módra
(**hol**shollaato sægædee **mā̄w**dro)

fish salad Szeged style: fish pieces, diced peppers, tomatoes and chives turned in oil and accompanied by lettuce and hard-boiled eggs

hideg fogas tartármártással
(**hee**dæg **faw**gosh **tort**aarmaartaash-shol)

kind of pike-perch with tartar sauce (mayonnaise with gherkins, chives, capers and olives)

paprika szeletek körözöttel töltve
(**pop**reeko **sæl**ætæk **kur**rurzurt-tæl turltvæ)

green peppers, sliced in four, filled with a mix of ewe's cheese, butter, mustard, paprika, caraway seeds and some beer

Bread and other bakery products

"The Hungarians will even eat bread with bread" goes an old saying—which may give you an idea of the varied and tasty range of bakery products you can look forward in this country. Most milk bars, beer halls and better restaurants automatically place a selection of them on your table when you order.

fodros fehér kalács (fawdrawsh fæhayr kollaach)	spongy white milk-bread, available as rolls or in slices	
mazsolás kalács (mozhawlaash kollaach)	spongy white milk-bread with raisins	
óriás kifli (a@wreeaash keeflee)	large, flaky, crescent-shaped roll	
paprikás stangli (popreekaash shtonglee)	paprika-seasoned bread finger, reddish in colour	
sajtos pogácsa (shoytawsh pawgaacho)	bread cone with cheese	
tepertős pogácsa (tæpærtūrsh pawgaacho)	crispy bread cone, slightly salted and peppered, with bacon pieces	
túrós karika (tōōra@wsh korreeko)	dough ring with curds	

Soups

Richly flavoured soups are part of the Hungarian way of life. They are generally quite thick. In some regions soup may be served for breakfast.

I'd like some soup.	**Levest kérek.**	læværsht kayræk
almaleves hidegen/ melegen	olmollæværsh heedægæn/ mælægæn	cold/hot apple soup
bajai halászlé	boyo-ee hollaaslay	fish and potato soup
burgonyakrémleves	boorgawn^yokraymlæværsh	cream of potato soup
csontleves	chawntlæværsh	bone consommé

erőleves húsgom- bóccal	ærūrlævæsh hōōshgawm- bāwtstsol	consommé with meat dumplings
gombaleves	gawmbollævæsh	mushroom soup
kalocsai halászlé	kollawcho-ee hollaaslay	fish soup in red wine
paradicsomleves	porroddeechawmlævæsh	tomato soup
savanyútojás leves	shovvon^Yōōtaw^Yaash lævæsh	sour egg soup
spárgakrém leves	shpaargokraym lævæsh	cream of asparagus soup
tejfeles bableves	tæ^Yfælæsh boblævæsh	bean soup with sour cream
vegyes gyümölcs- leves hidegen	væd^Yæsh d^Yewmurlchlæ- væsh heedægæn	chilled fruit soup

Soup specialities

bakonyi betyárleves
(bokkawn^Yee bæt^Yaarlævæsh)
"outlaw soup"—soup Bakony style: a mix of chicken, beef chunks, thin noodles, mushrooms and vegetables, richly spiced

gulyásleves
(gōōyaashlævæsh)
Hungarian goulash: a mix of beef chunks, potatoes, onions, tomatoes and peppers, richly spiced with paprika, caraway seeds and garlic

Jókai bableves
(yāwko-ee boblævæsh)
bean soup Jókai style (Jókai was a famous Hungarian writer): a mix of smoked pig's knuckles, butter beans and carrots, seasoned with pepper, garlic, paprika and parsley

kunsági pandúrleves
(koonshaaghee pondōōrlævæsh)
chicken or pigeon soup Kunság style: seasoned with paprika, grated nutmeg, ginger and garlic

magyaros bur- gonyaleves
(mod^Yorrawsh boorgawn^Yollævæsh)
Hungarian potato soup: diced potatoes and onions with paprika

magyaros csirke- aprólék leves
(mod^Yorrawsh cheer- kæoprāwlayk lævæsh)
Hungarian chicken giblet soup with mushrooms, diced potatoes, pepper rings and tomatoes

palócleves
(pollāwtslævæsh)
a mix of mutton, French beans, potatoes and sour cream, seasoned with paprika, garlic and caraway seeds

szegedi halászlé
(sægædee hollaaslay)
a mix of various kinds of fish (usually carp, pike and wels, tomato and pepper rings, with hot paprika seasoning

Fish

| I'd like some fish. | **Halat szeretnék.** | hollot særætnayk |
| What fish do you recommend? | **Milyen halat ajánl?** | mee^yæn hollott oyaanl |

csuka	chooko	pike
fogas	fawgosh	a local fish of the pike-perch family
harcsa	horcho	wels
kecsege	kæchægæ	sterlet
nyelvhal	n^yælvhol	sole
pisztráng	peestraang	trout
ponty	pawnt^y	carp
tőkehal	tūrkæhol	cod
tonhal	tawnhol	tunny (Am. tuna)

Fish specialities

csuka tejfölben sütve
(chooko tæ^yfurlbæn shewtvæ)

pike fried and served with sour cream

fogas fehér bormártásban
(fawgosh fæhayr bawrmaartaashbon)

fogas in a white-wine sauce

fogasszeletek Gundel módra
(fawgoshsælætæk goondæl māwdro)

slices of *fogas* Gundel style (Gundel was a famous Hungarian restaurateur): breaded fillet of pike

halfatányéros
(holfottaan^yayrawsh)

assorted fish, some breaded or fried, served on a wooden plate, accompanied by tartar sauce

harcsaszelet fűszermártásban
(horchossælæt fēwsæmaartaashbon)

fillet of wels in a spicy sauce doused with white wine

kecsege tejszínes paprikás mártásban
(kæchægæ tæ^ysēēnæsh popreekaash maartaashbon)

sterlet in a cream and paprika sauce

EATING OUT

paprikás ponty (popreekaash pawnt^y)	carp served in a paprika sauce
pisztráng tejszín mártásban (peestraang tæ^{y}ssēēn maartaashbon)	trout baked in cream
rostélyos töltött ponty (rawshtay^{y}awsh turlturt pawnt^y)	fried carp, stuffed with a mix of bread, fish liver or roe, egg and herbs

Other specialities from Hungary's lakes and rivers include:

békacomb gombával és rákkal (baykotsawmb gawmbaavol aysh raak-kol)	frog's legs with freshwater crab-meat and mush-rooms
békacomb paprikásan (baykotsawmb popreekaashon)	frog's legs in a paprika sauce
rákpörkölt (raakpurrkurlt)	broiled crab

Sauces

The sauces that accompany Hungarian dishes are distinctively flavoured to enhance the pleasures of the palate. (Contrary to widespread belief, spicy-hot preparations are not typical of the national cuisine.)

almamártás	olmommaartaash	apple sauce
bakonyi gombamártás	bokkawn^{y}ee gawmbommaartaash	mushroom sauce
ecetes torma	ætsætæsh tawrmo	horse-radish sauce
fehérhagyma mártás	fæhayrhod^{y}mo maartaash	onion sauce
fokhagymás mártás	fawkhod^{y}maash maartash	garlic sauce
kapormártás	koppawrmaartaash	dill sauce
meggymártás	mæd^{y}maartaash	morello sauce
paprikás mártás	popreekaash maartaash	paprika sauce
tárkonyos mártás	taarkawn^{y}awsh maartaash	tarragon sauce
vadasmártás	voddoshmaartaash	brown sauce

Meat

I'd like some ...	... kérek.	... kayræk
beef	**Marhahús**	morhoho͞osht
lamb	**Bárányhús**	baaraanYho͞osht
pork	**Disznóhús**	deesnawho͞osht
veal	**Borjúhús**	bawryo͞oho͞osht
borda	bawrdo	chop
comb	tsawmb	leg
fasírozott	foshe͞erawzawt	meatballs
filé	feelay	fillet
kolbászfélék	kawlbaasfaylayk	sausages
lapocka	loppawtsko	shoulder
máj	maaY	liver
nyelv	nYælv	tongue
sonka	shawnko	ham
szalonna	sollawn-no	bacon

boiled	**főve**	fūrvæ
braised	**dinsztelve**	deenstælvæ
breaded	**rántva**	raantvo
fried	**sütve**	shewtvæ
grilled	**roston sütve**	rawshtawn shewtvæ
roasted	**sülve**	shewlvæ
stewed (quickly)	**főzve**	fūrzvæ
stewed (slowly)	**pörköltnek**	purrkurltnæk
underdone (rare)	**félig nyersen**	fayleeg nYærshæn
medium	**közepesen kisütve**	kurzæpæshæn keeshewtvæ
well-done (fried)	**jól megsütve**	yāwl mægshewtvæ
well-done (boiled)	**jól megfőzve**	yāwl mægfūrzvæ

Veal

borjúpaprikás
(bawryo͞opopreekaash) — veal fricassée with onions, pepper rings, tomatoes and a seasoning of paprika and garlic

borjúpörkölt
(bawryo͞opurkurlt) — a stew composed of veal chunks, onions, tomatoes, pepper rings, seasoned with paprika and garlic

lecsós borjúmáj rántva
(læchāwsh bawryo͞omaaY raantvo) — breaded veal liver, garnished with a mix of pepper slices, tomatoes, rice, spiced with paprika and garlic

Beef

alföldi marharostélyos
(**olf**urldee **mor**horrawsh-tay^{Y}awsh)

steak Alföldi style: with a rich sauce and stewed vegetables

cigányrostélyos
(**tsee**gaan^Y-rawshtay^{Y}awsh)

steak gypsy style: with a brown sauce and braised vegetables

csikós tokány
(**chee**kāwsh **taw**kaan^Y)

strips or chunks of beef braised in a mix of bacon strips or bits, onion rings and sour cream and tomato concentrate

erdélyi tokány
(**ær**day^{Y}ee **taw**kaan^Y)

a dish originating in Transylvania: virtually the same as *csikós tokány*, but without the sour cream

hortobágyi rostélyos
(**hawr**tawbaad^{Y}ee rawshtay^{Y}awsh)

steak Hortobágy style: braised in a mix of stock and bacon bits and accompanied by a large semolina dumpling

Pork

erdélyi rakott-káposzta
(**ær**day^{Y}ee **ro**kkawtkaapawsto)

a Transylvanian dish consisting of layers of cabbage interspersed with rice and minced, spiced pork, covered with sour cream and baked in the oven

debreceni fatányéros
(**dæb**rætsænee **fo**ttaan^{Y}ayrawsh)

a Debrecen speciality, prepared only for parties of three or more, usually containing pork chops and choice fillets as well as some veal; garnished with lettuce

rablóhús nyárson
(**rob**lāwhōōsh n^Y**aar**shawn)

alternating pieces of pork, onions, mushrooms, bacon and veal roasted and served on a skewer

tejfölös-gombás sertésborda
(**tæ**^{Y}furlursh **gawm**baash **shær**tayshbawrdo)

pork chop with mushrooms and sour cream

töltött malac újfalusi módra
(**turl**turt **mo**llots ōō^Y**fol**looshee **mā**wdro)

stuffed suckling-pig Újfalu style: with a mix of spiced minced meat, liver, egg and bread

Game and fowl

I'd like some game.	**Vadasat szeretnék.**	voddoshot særaætnayk
csirke	cheerkæ	chicken
fácán	faatsaan	pheasant
fogoly	fawgaw[y]	partridge
galamb	gollomb	pigeon
kacsa	kocho	duck
kappan	kop-pon	capon
liba	leebo	goose
nyúl	n[y]ōōl	rabbit
őz	ūrz	venison
pulyka	poo[y]ko	turkey
vaddisznó	vod-deesnāw	wild boar
vadkacsa	vodkocho	wild duck
vadliba	vodleebo	wild goose

csabai szarvascomb
(**chobb**oee **sor**voshtsawmb)
venison stuffed with spicy Csabai sausage served in a paprika sauce

fácán gesztenyével töltött gombával
(**faatsaan** gætæn[y]-ayvæl **turl**turt **gawm**baavol)
pheasant with a mushroom and chestnut filling

fogoly szalonnában sütve
(**fawgaw**[y] **sol**lawn-naabon **shewt**væ)
partridge in a bacon envelope, served in a sauce of stock, tomato concentrate and seasoning

nyúlszeletek pirított szárnyasmájjal
(**n**[y]ōōlsælætæk **peerēē**tawt **saarn**[y]oshmaa[y]-yol)
rabbit with roasted chicken liver

pulykacomb tejfeles gombamártással
(**poo**[y]kotsawmb tæ[y]fælæsh **gawm**bommaartaash-shol)
turkey cutlet in a mushroom sauce

vaddisznó boróka-mártással
(**vod**-deesnāw **baw**rāwkommaartaash-shol)
wild boar served in a juniper sauce

Vegetables—Salads

Vegetables and salads are served along with the main course in set menus. Otherwise, you may order them separately from the bill of fare.

burgonya	boorgawn^yo	potatoes
fehérrépa	fæhayr-raypo	turnips
gomba	gawmbo	mushrooms
hagyma	hod^ymo	onions
káposzta	kaapawsto	cabbage
kelbimbó	kælbeembaw	Brussels sprouts
kelkáposzta	kælkaapawsto	cauliflower
kukorica	kookawreetso	type of sweetcorn
lencse	lænchæ	lentils
paprika	popreeko	pepper
paradicsom	porroddeechawm	tomatoes
saláta	shollaato	lettuce
sárgarépa	shaargorraypo	carrots
spárga	shpaargo	asparagus
spenót	shpænawt	spinach
sültkrumpli	shewltkroomplee	chips (French fries)
uborka	oobawrko	cucumber
vegyesfőzelék	væd^yæshfūrzælayk	mixed vegetables
vegyesköret	væd^yæshkur-ræt	mixed vegetables (served along with the dish)
zeller	zæl-lær	celery
zöldbab	zurldbob	French beans
zöldborsó	zurldbawrshaw	peas

Some herbs and spices used in Hungarian cooking:

édeskömény	aydæshkurmayn^y	caraway seeds
édespaprika	aydæshpopreeko	mild paprika
fokhagyma	fawkhod^ymo	garlic
fűszerpaprika	fēwsærpopreeko	chillies
kakukkfű	kokkookfēw	thyme
komló	kawmlaw	hops
majoránna	moyawraan-no	marjoram
pirospaprika	peerawshpopreeko	strong paprika
rozmaring	rawzmorreeng	rosemary
sáfrány	shaafraan^y	crocus leaf
szegfűszeg	sægfēwsæg	cloves
szekfűbors	sækfēwbawrsh	allspice
szerecsendió	særæchændeeaw	nutmeg

Desserts

The Hungarians have a decidedly sweet tooth and much to offer in the way of desserts.

I'd like a dessert, please.	**Egy adag deszertet kérek.**	æd^y oddog dæsærtæt kayræk
Something light, please.	**Valami könnyűt legyen szíves.**	vollommee kurn^{y}ewt læd^{y}æn seevæsh
Nothing more, thank you.	**Köszönöm, többet nem kérek.**	kursurnurm turb-bæt næm kayræk
almás palacsinta	olmaash pollocheento	apple pancake
aranygaluska	orron^{y}gollooshko	sweet dumpling
csokoládéfánk	chawkawlaadayfaank	chocolate doughnut
csúsztatott palacsinta	chōōstottawt pollocheento	multi-layer pancake
dobostorta	dawbawshtawrto	caramel-topped chocolate cream cake
gesztenyepüré tejszínhabbal	gæstæn^{y}æpewray tæ^{y}sseenhob-bol	chestnut purée with whipped cream
Gundel palacsinta	goondæl pollocheento	pancake with nut-cream and raisin filling, flambéd
kapros túrós rétes	koprawsh tōōrāwsh raytæsh	curds strudel with dill
kapucineres felfújt	koppootseenæræsh fælfōō^{y}t	chocolate soufflé
kecskeméti barack-puding	kæchkæmaytee borrotsk-"pudding"	apricot pudding with vanilla cream
képviselőfánk	kaypveeshælūrfaank	cream puff
máglyarakás	maag^{y}orrokkaash	apple and jam pudding
mákosrétes	maakawshraytæsh	poppy-seed strudel
mandula felfújt	mondoolo fælfōō^{y}t	almond soufflé
rakott palacsinta	rokkawt pollocheento	multi-layer pancakes with various fillings
somlói galuska	shawmlāwee gollooshko	sweet dumplings made with vanilla, nuts and chocolate, in an orange-and-rum sauce
sült derelye	shewlt dæræ^{y}æ	fried jam turn-over
szilvás rétes	seelvaash raytæsh	plum strudel
töltött alma	turlturt olmo	apple stuffed with vanilla, raisins and cream

Ice-cream

Ice-cream and parfaits are often available as desserts. In addition, pastry shops and milkbars serve a variety of imaginative ice-based creations, frequently including fruit, cream or fancy cakes. As a dessert, ice-cream is sometimes served with a fresh-fruit salad. Alternatively, it may be flambéd with rum. There will generally be a choice of flavours.

Have you any ice-cream?	**Van fagylaltjuk?**	von fod^ylolt^yook
banán	bonnaan	banana
citrom	tseetrawm	lemon
csokoládé	chawkawlaaday	chocolate
dió	deeāw	walnut
eper	æpær	strawberry
kávé	kaavay	coffee
málna	maalno	raspberry
meggy	maed^y	sour cherry
mogyoró	mawd^yawrāw	hazelnut
narancs	norronch	orange
pisztás	peestaash	pistachio
vanília	vonnēēleeo	vanilla
Could I have it flambéd?	**Kaphatok lángoló fagylaltot?**	kophottawk laangawlāw fod^yloltawt

Cheese

Though Hungary produces more than a hundred types of cheese, on the whole they range little in taste. Most are rather bland, but there are some spiced or smoked varieties. Imitation camembert, cheddar, Dutch edam and other foreign cheeses are also available in better restaurants.

Processed cheeses, conveniently packaged in tubes or the familiar individual triangular portions, may be flavoured with pepper, paprika or a variety of vegetable aromas.

I'd like some cheese.	**Sajtot szeretnék.**	shoytawt særætnayk
Do you have a cheese-board?	**Milyen sajt van?**	mee^yæn shoyt von

Fruit

Do you have fresh fruit?	**Van friss gyümölcsük?**	von freesh d^yewmurlchewk
What sort of fruit do you have?	**Milyen gyümölcsük van?**	mee^yæn d^yewmurlchewk von
I'd like a fresh-fruit cocktail.	**Friss gyümölcs-koktélt kérek.**	freesh d^yewmurlchkawk-taylt **kay**ræk

alma	olmo	apple
áfonya	aafawn^ya	blueberries
ananász	onnonnaas	pineapple
banán	bonnaan	banana
citrom	tseetrawm	lemon
császárkörte	chaassaarkurrtæ	type of pear
cseresznye	chæræsn^yæ	cherries
datolya	dottaw^yo	dates
dió	deeāw	chestnuts
egres	ægrāsh	gooseberries
eper	æpær	strawberries
fekete cseresznye	fækætæ chæræsn^yæ	heart cherries
fekete ribizli	fækætæ reebeezlee	blackcurrants
füge	fewgæ	figs
gesztenye	gæstæn^yæ	chestnuts
görögdinnye	gurrurgdeen^yæ	water melon
jonatán alma	yawnottaan olmo	Jonathan apple
körte	kurrtæ	pear
málna	maalno	raspberries
mandarin	mondoreen	tangerine
mandula	mondoolo	almonds
meggy	mæd^y	sour cherries
mogyoró	mawd^yawrāw	hazelnuts
narancs	norronch	orange
őszibarack	ūrseeborrotsk	peach
ribizli	reebeezlee	redcurrants
ringló	reenglāw	greengage
sárgabarack	shaargobborrotsk	apricot
sárgadinnye	shaargoddeen^yæ	honeydew melon
starking alma	shtorkeeng olmo	starking apple
szeder	sædær	mulberries
szilva	seelvo	plum
szőlő	sūrlūr	grapes

The bill (check)

I'd like the bill, please.	**Kérem a számlát.**	kayræm o saamlaat
We'd like to pay separately.	**Külön-külön kívánunk fizetni.**	kewlurn kewlurn kēēvaanoonk feezætnee
What is this amount for?	**Ez mire vonatkozik?**	æz meeræ vawnotkawzeek
You've made a mistake in this bill, I think.	**Azt hiszem, ez a számla hibás.**	ost heessæm æz o saamlo heebash
Is everything included?	**Minden szerepel a számlában?**	meendæn særæpæl o saamlaabon

A FELSZOLGÁLÁSI DÍJ AZ ÁRAKBAN BENNFOGLALTATIK

SERVICE INCLUDED

How much do I owe you?	**Mennyi a számla összege?**	mæn^Yee o saamlo urssægæ
Do you accept traveller's cheques?	**Fizethetek traveller's csekkel?**	feezæt-hætæk trovvæl-lærs chæk-kæl
Can I pay with this credit card?*	**Fizethetek ezzel a hitelkártyával?**	feezæt-hætæk æz-zæl o heetælkaart^Yaavol
Thank you, this is for you.	**Köszönöm. Ez a magáé.**	kursurnurm. æz o moggaa-ay
Keep the change.	**A többi a magáé.**	o turb-bee o moggaa-ay
That was an excellent/ delicious meal.	**Az étel kiváló/ fínom volt.**	oz aytæl keevaalāw/ fēēnawm vawlt
We've enjoyed ourselves very much, thank you.	**Jól szórakoztunk.**	yāwl sāwrokkawztoonk

---

* In Hungary, credit cards are generally accepted in all establishments frequented by foreign tourists.

Complaints

But perhaps you'll have something to complain about:

English	Hungarian	Pronunciation
That's not what I ordered.	Nem ezt rendeltem.	næm æst rændæltæm
I asked for...	Én...-t rendeltem.	ayn ...-t rændæltæm
I asked for a small portion (for the child).	Egy kisadagot rendeltem (a gyereknek).	æd^y keeshoddoggawt rændæltæm (o d^{y}æræknæk)
There must be some mistake.	Itt valami félre-értés lesz.	eet vollommee faylræayr-taysh læs
May I change this?	Hozna valami mást helyette?	hawzno vollommee maasht hæ^{y}æt-tæ
The meat is...	A húst...	o hōōsht
overdone	agyonsütötték	od^{y}awnshewturt-tayk
underdone	csak félig sütötték meg	chok fayleeg shewturt-tayk mæg
This is too...	Ez nagyon...	æz nod^{y}awn
bitter	keserű	kæshærēw
salty	sós	shāwsh
sour	savanyú	shovvon^{y}ōō
sweet	édes	aydæsh
The food is cold.	Ez az étel hideg.	æz oz aytæl heedæg
It's not fresh.	Ez nem friss.	æz næm freesh
What's taking you so long?	Mi tart ilyen sokáig?	mee tort ee^{y}æn shawkaa-eeg
Have you forgotten our drinks?	Az innivalókat elfelejtette?	oz een-neevollāwkot ælfælæ^{y}tæt-tæ
The wine is too cold.	A bor túl hideg.	a bawr tōōl heedæg
The wine tastes of cork.	Ez a bor dugóízű.	æz o bawr doogāwēēzēw
The beer isn't chilled.	A sör nincs behűtve.	o shurr neench bæhēwtvæ
This beer is flat.	Ez a sör állott.	æz o shurr aal-lawt
This isn't clean.	Ez nem tiszta.	æz næm teesto
There's a draught here.	Huzat van.	hoozot von
Would you ask the headwaiter to come over?	Kérem, hívja ide a főpincért!	kayræm hēēvyo eedæ o fūrpeenchayrt

Drinks

| Give me the drinks card, please. | **Legyen szíves az itallapot idehozni!** | læd^yæn sēēvæsh oz eetol-loppawt eedæhawznee |

Beer

Both local beer (which is rather strong) and foreign brands are usually available. It may be sold by the bottle or on draught. A 3-decilitre glass is called a *pohár*, a half-litre mug a *korsó*.

I'd like a bottle of ... beer.	**Egy üveg ... sört kérnék.**	æd^y ewvæg shurrt kayrnayk
German	**német**	naymæt
Hungarian	**magyar**	mod^yor
Pilsen	**pilzeni**	peelzænee
dark/light	**barna/világos**	borno/veelaagawsh
A *pohár/korsó* of beer, please.	**Egy pohár/korsó sört kérek.**	æd^y pawhaar/kawrshāw shurrt kayræk

> **EGÉSZSÉGÉRE!**
> (ægayssaygayræ)
>
> CHEERS!

Wine

For its size, Hungary produces an impressive range of good wines.

What kind of wine do you have?	**Milyen boruk van?**	mee^yæn bawrook von
I'd like a ... of wine.	**Egy ... bort kérek.**	æd^y ... bawrt kayræk
glass/bottle	**pohár/üveg**	pawhaar/ewvæg
A bottle of red/white wine, please.	**Egy üveg fehér/vörös bort kérek.**	æd^y ewvæg fæhayr/vurrursh bawrt kayræk

FLUID MEASURES: see page 130

Type of wine	Examples	Accompanies
sweet white wine	Balatonfüredi szemelt rizling, Csopaki olasz rizling, Akali zöldszilváni, Tokaji aszu	desserts and pastry, but also thick soups
light dry white wine	Badacsonyi kéknyelű, Badacsonyi szürkebarát, Badacsonyi zöldszilváni, Egri Leányka, Tokaji furmint, Tokaji szamorodni	fish meals, liver, lighter meat dishes, goulash and other stews, steaks, cold meats, fruit
light-bodied red wine	Vaskúti kadarka, Villányi burgundi, Villányi kadarka, Egri pinot noir	fish soups, veal, pork, lamb, ham, beef, fowl, game, cheese
full-bodied red wine	Egri bikavér, Villányi medoc noir, Tihanyi merlot	game, duck, cheese
sparkling wine (sweet)	Törley réserve, Pannonia	desserts and fruit
sparkling wine (dry)	Pompadur, Pannonia	fowl, game
sparkling wine (extra dry)	Pannonia dry	light cheese

Tokay wine

This world-famous wine comes from the area near the city of Tokaj, considered by many the country's most outstanding wine-growing region. Its excellence is attributed to the properties of the local soil, the mineral content of the water, the traditional production methods employed and, some local people insist, the peculiar quality of the sunshine there.

Tokay wines come in three different categories: *Tokaji furmint* (dry), *Tokaji szamorodni* (medium-sweet) and *Tokaji aszu* (full-bodied, very sweet). Tokay vintages are graded according to excellence on a scale of from 3 to 5 *puttonyos* or points.

Other alcoholic drinks

Cocktails and highballs are unfamiliar to most Hungarians, and you are unlikely to find any available in ordinary restaurants and drinking places. Imported spirits can be found in some better bars and restaurants.

Do you have any...?	Van...?	von
cognac	konyakjuk	kawn^yokyook
gin	dzsinjük	dzheenyewk
liqueur	likörjük	leekurr^yewk
rum	rumjuk	roomyook
vermouth	vermutjuk	værmootyook
whisky	viszkijük	veeskee^vewk
vodka	vodkájuk	vawdkaa^vook
A (double) whisky, please.	Egy (dupla) viszkit, kérek.	æd^y (dooplo) veeskeet kayræk
neat (straight)	tisztán	teestaan
on the rocks	jéggel kérem	yayg-gæl kayræm
with a little water	kevés vízzel	kævaysh vēēz-zæl
Give me a gin and tonic, please.	Egy adag dzsint kérek tonikkal.	æd^y oddog dzheent kayræk tawneek-kol
Just a dash of soda, please.	Csak egy csöpp szódával kérem.	chok æd^y churp sāwdaavol kayræm
2 rum-and-cokes, please.	2 rumot kérek kólával.	2 roomawt kayræk kāwlaavol

For a change, you might like to try one of Hungary's excellent fruit brandies:

I'd like a glass of... brandy.	Kérek egy pohár... pálinkát.	kayræk æd^y pawhaar... paaleenkaat
apple	alma	olmo
apricot	barack	borrotsk
cherry	cseresznye	chæræsnæ
pear	körte	kurtæ
plum	szilva	seelvo

A potent concoction you are unlikely to want to order but may be offered is a "Puszta cocktail"—a mixture of three kinds of fruit brandies and vermouth, served with lemon and iced. Treat it with respect!

Soft drinks

Some international soft-drink brands are widely available, along with a variety of fruit juices. Bottled mineral water, usually sparkling, is on sale everywhere.

I'd like some...	... kérek.	... kayræk
apple juice	Almalevet	olmollævæt
apricot juice	Baracklét	borrotsklayt
cola drink	Kólát	kāwlaat
fruit juice	Gyümölcslevet	d^{y}ewmurlchlævæt
grapefruit juice	Grépfruit-lét	"grapefruit" layt
lemonade	Limonádét	leemawnaadayt
lemon juice	Citromlét	tseetrawmlayt
mineral water	Ásvány vizet	aashvaan^y veezæt
orange juice	Narancslét	norronchlayt
soda water	Szóda vizet	sāwdo veezæt
tomato juice	Paradicsomlét	porroddeechawmlayt

Coffee and tea

As you come to notice the Hungarians drinking coffee at all hours of the day, you'll be able to believe that the nation's per-capita consumption is one of the world's highest. Coffee is drunk strong (espresso style), black, usually sweet and very hot—though you obviously need not follow the local custom if you prefer your coffee otherwise. At most places, even white breakfast coffee is based on espresso.

Tea in Hungary is generally found rather weak and tasteless by British and American visitors.

I'd like a small/ large coffee.	Egy szimpla/dupla kávét kérek.	æd^y seemplo/dooplo kaavayt kayræk
A white coffee, please.	Egy tejeskávét kérek.	æd^y tæ^{y}æshkaavayt kayræk
A cup of tea, please.	Egy csésze teát kérek.	æd^y chayssæ tæaat kayræk
Please bring me some ...	... kérem.	... kayræm
cream/milk	Krémmel/Tejjel	kraym-mæl/tæ^{y}yæl
lemon/sugar	Citrommal/Cukorral	tseetrawm-mol/tsookawr-rol

Eating light—Snacks

For a quick sit-down meal, go to a *bisztro, büfé, cukrászda, önkiszolgáló, tejivó* or *tejbár* (see pages 38–39).

I'll have one of those, please.	**Egy ilyet kérek.**	æd^y ee^yæt kayræk
biscuits	**apró sütemény**	opraw shewtæmayn^y
bread	**kenyér**	kæn^yayr
cakes	**tea sütemény**	tæo shewtæmayn^y
cheese	**sajt**	shoyt
chicken	**csirke**	cheerkæ
half a roasted chicken	**fél gril csirke**	fayl "grill" cheerkæ
chips	**sült krumpli**	shewlt kroomplee
chocolate	**tábla csokoládé**	taablo chawkawlaaday
frankfurters	**pár virsli**	paar veershlee
French fries	**sült krumpli**	shewlt kroomplee
fried doughnut	**lángos**	laangawsh
fried eggs	**tükörtojás**	tewkurrtaw^yaash
fried fish	**sült hal**	shewlt hol
fried potato slices	**roseibni**	rawshæeebnee
fried sausages	**sült kolbász**	shewlt kawlbaass
ham and eggs	**sonkát tojással**	shawnkaat taw^yaash-shol
ham sandwich	**sonkás szendvics**	shawnkaash sændveech
ice-cream	**fagylalt**	fod^ylolt
ketchup	**ketchup**	kæchurp
meat sandwich	**húsos szendvics**	hooshaws sændveech
mustard	**mustár**	moshtaar
salami sandwich	**szalámis szendvics**	sollaameesh sændveech
sandwich	**szendvics**	sændveech
scrambled eggs	**rántotta**	raantawt-to
sweetcorn	**kukorica**	kookawreetso

beetroot :   *cékla*   *tsiklo .*

DRINKS: see page 60

Travelling around

Plane

Budapest Ferihegy is the country's only commercial airport.
There are, therefore, no scheduled domestic flights. Airport
staff mostly speak some English or German, but here are a
few useful expressions, just in case:

Is there a flight to Vienna?	**Van Bécsbe járatuk?**	von **baychbæ yaa**rottook
When is the next plane to London?	**Mikor indul a következő gép Londonba?**	**mee**kawr **een**dool o **kur**vætkæzūr gayp **lawn**dawnbo
Is it nonstop?	**Leszállás nélkül?**	**læs**saal-laash **nayl**kewl
Can I make a connection to New York?	**Át tudok szállni egy Nju-jork-i gépre?**	aat **too**dawk **saal**nee æd^y n^{y}oo-yawrk-ee **gayp**ræ
I'd like a ticket to Rome.	**Rómába kérek egy jegyet.**	**rāw**maabo **kay**ræk æd^y **yæd**^{y}æt
What's the fare ...?	**Mennyibe kerül egy jegy ...?**	**mæn**^{y}eebæ **kæ**rewl æd^y **yæd**^{y}
single (one-way)	**egy irányban**	æd^y **eer**aan^{y}bon
return (roundtrip)	**oda-vissza**	**aw**do **vees**-so
economy class	**turista osztályon**	**too**reeshto **aws**taa^{y}awn
first class	**első osztályon**	**æl**shūr **aws**taa^{y}awn
When is the departure time?	**Mikor indul a járat?**	**mee**kawr **een**dool o **yaa**rot
What time do I have to check in?	**Mikor kell bejelentkeznem?**	**mee**kawr kæl bæ^{y}ælænt**kæz**næm
What's the flight number?	**Mi a járat száma?**	mee o **yaa**rot **saa**mo
What time do we arrive?	**Mikor érkezünk meg?**	**mee**kawr **een**dool o **yaa**rot

ÉRKEZÉS	INDULÁS
ARRIVAL	DEPARTURE

TELLING THE TIME: see page 178

Train

The Hungarian State Railways maintain quite a dense rail network, partly electrified, with both first- and second-class seating. First-class compartments, marked I, are comfortable. Second-class compartments, marked II, are adequate but not always as clean as they might be; they are also likely to be rather crowded and noisy. Service is punctual. International connections are generally good.

Rail travel within Hungary is quite inexpensive and is an excellent way to get to see the country. Hungary is linked to the Inter Rail agreement which allows young people up to the age of 25 to travel throughout some thirty countries of Europe for one month at a low-cost flat-rate charge. Travel agents in all Western European countries have details.

For trips within Hungary, tickets can be purchased from railway stations and travel agencies. A variety of options exist—regular, excursion, trade-fair and student tickets.

The three main railway stations in Budapest are: *Nyugati* (West), *Déli* (South) and *Keleti* (East). At all of them, some staff speak a little English or German.

Type of trains

Nemzetközi gyorsvonat (næmzætkurzee dᵛawrshvawnot)	International express with first- and second-class seating; advance reservation (at an extra charge) is highly advisable.
Sebesvonat (shæbæshvawnot)	Express train, stopping at major centres only.
Gyorsvonat (dᵛawrshvawnot)	A domestic express train which stops more frequently.
Személyvonat (sæmayᵛvawnot)	Slow train, stopping at all stations.
Helyiérdekű (hæᵛeeayrdækēw)	Suburban train, painted green, often integrated into the municipal public transport system.
Motorvonat (mawtawrvawnot)	Rail coach, diesel, comprising three or four cars, used for shorter distances.

TRAVELLING AROUND

To the railway station

Where's the railway station?	**Hol a vasútállomás?**	hawl o voshōōtaal-lawmaash
Taxi, please!	**Halló, taxi!**	hol-lāw toxee
Take me to the ... Station.	**Vigyen kérem a ... pályaudvarra.**	veed^{Y}æn kayræm o ... paa^{Y}o-oodvor-ro
East	**keleti**	kælætee
South	**déli**	daylee
West	**nyugati**	n^{Y}oogottee
Which bus goes to the ... Station?	**Melyik busz megy a ... pályaudvarra?**	mæ^{Y}eek booss mæd^Y o ... paa^{Y}o-oodvor-ro

---

| **FELVILÁGOSITÁS** | INFORMATION |
| **VALUTABEVÁLTÁS** | CURRENCY EXCHANGE |

Where's the ...?

Where is the ...?	**Hol van ...?**	hawl von
currency exchange office	**a valutabeváltó hely**	o vollootobbævaaltāw hæ^Y
information office	**az információs iroda**	oz eenfawrmaatseeāwsh eerawdo
letter box	**a postaláda**	o pawshtollaado
lost-property (lost-and-found) office	**az elhagyott tárgyak irodája**	oz ælhod^{Y}awt taard^{Y}ok eerawdaa^{Y}o
luggage lockers	**a csomagmegőrző**	o chawmogmægūrzūr
newsstand	**az újságos kioszk**	oz ōō^{Y}shaagawsh keeawsk
platform 5	**az 5-ödik peron**	oz 5 urdeek pærawn
restaurant	**az étterem**	oz ayt-tæræm
snack bar	**a gyorsbüfé**	o d^{Y}awrshbewfay
ticket office	**a jegypénztár**	o yæd^{Y}paynztaar
travel agency	**az utazási iroda**	oz ootozzaashee eerawdo
waiting room	**a váróterem**	o vaarāwtæræm
Where are the toilets?	**Hol vannak az illemhelyek?**	hawl von-nok oz eel-læmhæ^{Y}æk

TAXI: see page 27

Inquiries

When is the ... train to Siófok?	Mikor megy ... vonat Siófokra?	meekawr mæd^y ... vawnot sheeaw̅fawkro
first	az első	oz ælshūr
last	a következő	o kurvætkæzūr
next	az utolsó	oz ootawlshaw̅
What time does the train for Pécs leave?	Mikor indul a vonat Pécsre?	meekawr eendool o vawnot paychræ
What's the fare to Szeged?	Mibe kerül egy jegy Szegedig?	meebæ kærewl æd^y yæd^y sægædeeg
Is it an express train?	Ez gyorsvonat?	æz d^yawrshvawnot
What time does the train arrive at Győr?	Mikor érkezik meg a vonat Győrből?	meekawr ayrkæzeek mæg o vawnot d^yūrbūrl
Does the train stop at Hévíz?	Megáll a vonat Hévizen?	mægaal o vawnot hayveezæn
Is there a dining car on the train?	Van ezen a vonaton étkezőkocsi?	von æzæn o vawnottawn aytkæzūrkawchee
What platform does the train for Vienna leave from?	A bécsi gyorsvonat melyik vágányról indul?	a baychee d^yawrsh-vawnot mæ^yeek vaagaan^yraw̅l eendool

---

Vonat indul ...-ra/-re ... órakor.	There's a train to ... at ...
Ez egy gyorsvonat.	It's an express train.
... nál/nél át kell szállnia.	You have to change at ...
... nál/nél szálljon át és utazzon tovább egy helyi vonattal.	Change at ... and get a local train.
A 6. peron ...	Platform 6 is ...
ott/lent balra/jobbra	over there/downstairs on the left/right
Az ön vonata a ...-odik/ -edik vágányról indul.	Your train leaves from platform ...
... perces késéssel indul.	There's a delay of ... minutes.

NUMBERS: see page 175

Tickets

I'd like a ticket to Keszthely.	**Kérek egy jegyet Keszthelyre.**	kayræk æd^V yæd^{V}æt kæsthæ^{Y}ræ
single (one-way)	**egy útra**	æd^V ōōtro
return (roundtrip)	**oda-vissza**	awdo vees-so
first class	**első osztályra**	ælshūr awstaa^{Y}ro
second class	**második osztályra**	maashawdeek awstaa^{Y}ro
I'd like to make a seat reservation.	**Szeretnék helyjegyet váltani.**	særætnayk hæ^{Y}yæd^{V}æt vaaltonnee
I'd like a timetable, please.	**Kérek egy menetrendet.**	kayræk æd^V mænætrændæt

Első vagy második osztályra?	First or second class?
Egy útra vagy oda-vissza?	Single (one way) or return (roundtrip)?
10 éves korig a gyerekek félárú jeggyel utaznak.	It's half fare up to age 10.

Baggage—Porters

Porter!	**Hordár!**	hawrdaar
Take my luggage to the ... train.	**Kérem, vigye a csomagjaimat a ...-i vonathoz.**	kayræm veed^{V}æ o chawmog^{Y}o-eemot o ...-ee vawnot-hawz
Can I have this luggage registered?	**Ezeket a podgyászokat szeretném feladni.**	æzækæt o pawd^{V}assawkot særætnaym fælodnee
Where can I find a baggage trolley?	**Hol találhatok podgyász kézikocsit?**	hawl tollalhottawk pawd^{Y}ass kazeekawcheet

BEJÁRAT	ENTRANCE
KIJÁRAT	EXIT
A VÁGÁNYOKHOZ	TO THE PLATFORMS

BAGGAGE and PORTERS: see also page 24

TRAVELLING AROUND

All aboard

Does the train for Budapest leave from this platform?	A Budapestre menő vonat erről a peronról indul?	o boodoppæshtræ mænūr vawnot ær-rūl o pærawn-rāwl eendool
Is this the train for Debrecen?	Ez a debreceni vonat?	æz o dæbrætsænee vawnot
Is this seat taken?	Ez a hely foglalt?	æz o hæ^y fawglolt
I think that's my seat.	Azt hiszem, ez az én helyem.	ost heessæm æz oz ayn hæ^{y}æm
Would you mind looking after my luggage for a moment?	Vigyázna kérem egy percre a podgyászomra?	veed^{y}aazno kayræm æd^y pærtsræ o pawd-d^{y}aassawmro
Do you mind if I open/close the window?	Kinyithatnám/ Becsukhatnám az ablakot?	keen^{y}eet-hotnaam/ bæchook-hotnaam oz oblokkawt
Would you let me know before we get to Szeged?	Szólna, mielőtt Szegedre érkezünk?	sāwlno meeælūrt sægædræ ayrkæzewnk
What station is this?	Ez milyen állomás?	æz mee^{y}æn aal-lawmaash
How long does the train stop here?	Meddig áll itt a vonat?	mæd-deeg aal eet o vawnot
When do we get to the border?	Mikor, érkezünk a határra?	meekawr ayrkæzewnk o hottaar-ro

TILOS A DOHÁNYZÁS NO SMOKING	**DOHÁNYZÓ** SMOKING ALLOWED

Eating

Long-distance expresses, both domestic and international, have dining cars which serve meals at normal hours. On some trains, alcoholic drinks and light refreshments are also served at a buffet, or an attendant may come round with baskets of supplies.

Where's the dining car?	Merre van az étkezőkocsi?	mær-ræ von oz aytkæzūr-kawchee

MEAL TIMES: see page 40

Sleeping

Are there any free compartments in the sleeping car?	**Van még szabad hely a hálókocsiban?**	von mayg sobbod hæ^y o haalāw̄kawcheebon
Are there any couchettes available?	**Van még szabad kusettjük?**	von mayg sobbod kooshæt^yewk
Where's my berth?	**Melyik az én ágyam?**	mæ^yeek oz ayn aad^yom
Compartments 10 and 11, please.	**A 10-es és 11-es fülkéket kérem.**	o 10-æsh 11-æsh fewl-kaykæt kayræm
I'd like an upper/lower berth.	**Felső/Alsó ágyat kérek.**	fælshūr/olshāw̄ aad^yot kayræk
Would you make up our berths, please?	**Kérem, vesse meg az ágyamat.**	kayræm væsh-shæ mæg oz aad^yommot
Would you call me at 7 o'clock?	**Kérem, keltsen fel 7 órakor.**	kayræm kæltshæn fæl 7 āw̄rokkawr
Would you please bring me tea/coffee in the morning?	**Kérem, reggel hozzon teát/kávét.**	kayræm ræg-gæl hawz-zawn tæaat/kaavayt

Lost property

We hope you'll never need this section during your journey, but just in case:

Where's the lost-property (lost-and-found) office?	**Hol van a talált tárgyak irodája?**	hawl von o tollaalt taard^yok eerawdaayo
I've lost my ...	**Elvesztettem ...**	ælvæstæt-tæm
handbag	**a kézitáskámat**	o kayzeetaashkaamot
passport	**az útlevelemet**	oz ōōtlævælæmæt
ring	**a gyűrűmet**	o d^yēw̄rēw̄mæt
ticket	**a jegyemet**	o yæd^yæmæt
wallet	**az irattárcámat**	oz eerot-taartsaamot
watch	**az órámat**	oz āw̄raamot
I lost it in ...	**... -ban/-ben hagytam el.***	...-bon/-bæn hod^ytom æl
It's very valuable.	**Nagyon értékes.**	nod^yawn ayrtaykæsh

* See Grammar section for word endings.

Intercity coach (bus) services

Hungary has an extensive intercity coach network reaching into all parts of the country. Vehicles are comfortable and service is reasonably rapid, making bus travel the preferred means of transport of many. Prices are on a par with those for first-class rail travel. Most coaches are operated by the Volán and Mavaut companies. They are generally painted yellow.

Where can I get a coach to Esztergom?	Hol érem el az Esztergomba induló autóbuszt?	hawl ayræm æl oz æs-tærgawmbo eendoolāw oootāwboost
Which coach must I take for Tiszafüred?	Melyik busszal jutok el Tiszafüredre?	mæ\(^y\)eek boos-sol yootawk æl teessoffewrædræ
Where's the coach station?	Hol van az autóbusz állomás?	hawl von oz oootāwbooss aalawmaash
When is the ... coach to Győr?	Mikor indul ... busz Győrbe?	meekawr eendool ... booss d\(^y\)ūrrbæ
first	az első	oz ælshūr
last	az utolsó	oz ootawlshāw
next	a következő	o kurvætkæzūr
Do I have to change coaches?	Át kell közben szállnom?	aat kæl kurzbæn saal-nawm
I'd like a timetable, please.	Kérek egy menetrendet.	kayræk æd\(^y\) mænætræn-dæt

Urban public transport

The nation's larger towns have well-organized public transport services consisting of bus, tram (streetcar) and/or suburban train networks. Buses are blue, trams yellow, and suburban trains green. In addition, Budapest has an underground (subway) system.

Though the first underground (subway) on the continent of Europe was built in Budapest, large-scale construction was only taken up about 1950. There are now four lines in operation.

Modern, clean rolling stock serves the most important points throughout the capital. Stations are marked with a large M sign and a route number.

City buses, trams, suburban trains and the underground operate variously between 4 a.m. and midnight. On the underground, frequency of service is regulated to conform to passenger demand.

Smoking is prohibited on all urban public transport vehicles.

Tickets for buses, trams and the underground are on sale at termini, major news-stands, tobacconists' shops and post offices—but not on board the vehicles themselves. For the underground, you can also drop one Forint coin in a slot at the station entrance. Tickets for suburban trains must be purchased at the railway station.

Rates for suburban trains vary according to the distance travelled. Buses, trams and the underground each charge a—slightly different—flat rate for a ticket which is valid only on the one vehicle (no transfers). You must punch your ticket in the automatic machine on board (or, for the underground, at the station entrance).

Season tickets, valid on all four forms of urban public transport, are available for one-month periods only. However, if you are likely to be making extensive use of public transport facilities you might still find that their convenience outweighs the extra cost, even for a stay of only a few days—particularly in Budapest.

Inspectors make spot-checks on tickets, and you can expect quite a hefty fine if yours is not in order.

Where can I buy a ticket for the ...?	**Hol vehetek jegyet ...?**	hawl væhætæk ... yæd^yæt
bus	**az autóbuszra**	oz oootāwboosro
tram	**a villamosra**	o **veel**-lommawshro
suburban train	**a H.É.V.-re**	o hayv-ræ
underground (subway)	**a metróra**	o mætrāwro

A ... ticket, please.	Egy ... jegyet kérek.	æd^y ... yæd^{y}æt kayræk
bus/tram/ underground	autóbusz/villamos/ metró	ooootawbooss/veel- lommawsh/mætrāw
I'd like a season ticket, please.	Szeretnék egy bérletet váltani.	særætnayk æd^y bayrlæ- tæt vaaltonnee
Where's the nearest underground station?	Hol van a legköze- lebbi metró megálló?	hawl von o lægkurzælæb- bee mætrāw mægaal- lāw

Boats

For a change of pace and viewpoint, you might like to take one of the passenger boats which ply the Danube and Tisza rivers all year round. Or, during the summer months, you can go for a relaxing cruise on Lake Balaton. From May to September there is a daily hydrofoil service on the Danube between Budapest and Vienna which takes about five hours. Also during the summer season, a number of river excursion boats operate on the Danube leaving from Budapest Central Docks *(Vigadó-tér)*.

| A ... ticket to Vienna, please. | ... jegyet kérek Bécsbe. | ... yæd^{y}æt kayræk baychbæ |
| boat/hydrofoil | Hajó/Szárnyashajó | hoyāw/saarn^{y}oshhoyāw |

Other modes of transport

car	autó	ooootāw
bicycle	kerékpár	kæraykpaar
moped (motorbike)	moped	mawpæd
motorcycle	motorkerékpár	mawtawrkæraykpaar
pedalo	vizi biciklizni	veezee beetseekleeznee
rowing boat	evezős csónak	ævæzūrsh chāwnok
sailing boat	vitorlás	veetawrlaash
scooter	robogó	rawbawgāw

Or perhaps you prefer:

hitch-hiking	autóstoppal utazni	ooootāwshtawp-pol ootoznee
horse-riding	lovagolni	lawvoggawlnee
walking	gyalogolni	d^{y}ollawgawlnee

Around and about—Sightseeing

In this section we are more concerned with cultural attractions. For entertainment, see page 81.

If you want to buy a guide book, ask:

Can you recommend a good guide book on Budapest?	Ajánlana Budapestről egy jó utikalauzt?	oyaanlonno boodoppæsht-rūrl æd^y yāw ooteekollo-oozt
Is there a tourist office here?	Van itt utazási iroda?	von eet ootozzaashee eerawdo
Where's the tourist office?	Hol van az utazási iroda?	hawl von oz ootozzaashee eerawdo
What are the main points of interest?	Melyek a fő nevezetességek?	mæ^yæk o fūr nævæzætæsh-shaygæk
We're here for …	… vagyunk itt.	… vod^yoonk eet
only a few hours	Csak egy pár óráig	chok æd^y paar āwraaeeg
a day	Egy napig	æd^y noppeeg
3 days	3 napig	3 noppeeg
a week	Egy hétig	æd^y hayteeg
Can you recommend a sightseeing tour?	Ajánlana egy városnéző kőrútat?	oyaanlonno æd^y vaarawsh-nayzūr kūrrōōtot
Where does the bus start from?	Honnan indul az autóbusz?	hawn-non eendool oz oootāwbooss
Will it pick us up at the hotel?	A busz a szállodánál vesz fel bennünket?	o booss o saal-lawdaa-naal væs fæl bæn-newnkæt
Where do the cruises start from?	Honnan indul a kíránduló hajó?	hawn-non eendool o kēēraandoolāw hoyāw
What bus/underground do we take?	Melyik buszra/földalattira szálljunk fel?	mæ^yeek boosro/furld-ollot-teero saalyoonk fæl
How much does the tour cost?	Mennyibe kerül a városnéző kőrút?	mæn^yeebæ kærewl o vaarawshnayzūr kūrrōōt
What time does the tour start?	Mikor kezdődik a városnéző kőrút?	meekawr kæzdūrdeek o vaarawshnayzūr kurrōōt

TELLING THE TIME: see page 178

At what time do we get back?	Mikor érkezünk vissza?	meekawr ayrkæzewnk vees-so
Is lunch included in the tour price?	Az ebéd benne van az árban?	oz æbayd bæn-næ von oz aarbon
Is there an English-speaking guide?	Van angolul beszélő idegenvezetőjük?	von ongawlool bæsaylūr eedægænvæzætūryewk
We'd like to hire a car for the day.	Gépkocsit szeretnénk kölcsönözni egy napra.	gaypkawcheet særætnaynk kurlchurnurznee æd^y nopro
I'd like to hire a chauffeur-driven car.	Szeretnék bérelni egy kocsit sofőrrel.	særætnayk bayrælnee æd^y kawcheet shawfūrr-ræl
Can you get me an English-speaking chauffeur?	Kaphatnék egy angolul beszélő sofőrt?	kophotnayk æd^y ongawlool bæsaylūr shawfūrrt
I'd like to hire an English-speaking private guide.	Szeretnék külön, angolul beszélő idegenvezetőt kapni.	særætnayk kewlurn ongawlool bæsaylūr eedægænvæzætūrt kopnee
for half a day for a full day	fél napra egy napra	fayl nopro æd^y nopro
What will that cost me?	Mennyibe kerül?	mæn^yeebæ kærewl
Is that price all-inclusive?	Az árban minden benne van?	oz aarbon meendæn bæn-næ von
Can I pay with ...?	Fizethetek ...?	feezæt-hætæk
this credit card traveller's cheques	hitelkártyával traveller's csekkel	heetælkaart^yaavol trovvæl-lærs chæk-kæl
Where is/are the ...?	Hol van ...?	hawl von
airport	a repülőtér	o ræpewlūrtayr
art gallery	a képzőművészeti galéria	o kaypzūrmēwvayssætee gollayreeo
botanical gardens	a botanikus kert	o bawtonneekoosh kært
building	az épület	oz aypewlæt
business district	az üzleti negyed	oz ewzlætee næd^yæd
castle	a vár	o vaar
cathedral	a székesegyház	o saykæshæd^yhaaz
caves	a barlang	o borlong
cemetery	a temető	o tæmætūr
chapel	a kápolna	o kaapawlno
church	a templom	o tæmplawm
city centre	a városközpont	o vaarawshkurzpawnt

concert hall	a hangversenyterem	o hongværshæn^ytæræm
conference centre	a konferencia központ	o kawnfæræntseeo kurzpawnt
docks	a móló	o mawlaw
downtown area	a városközpont	o vaarawshkurzpawnt
exhibition	a kiállítás	o keeaal-leetaash
fortress	az erődítmény	oz ærūrdeetmayn ^y
fountain	a forrás	o fawr-raash
garden	a kert	o kært
lake	a tó	o taw
law courts	a bíróság	o beerawshaag
library	a könyvtár	o kurn^yvtaar
market	a piac	o peeots
memorial	az emlékoszlop	oz æmlaykawslawp
monument	az emlékmű	oz æmlaykmew
museum	a múzeum	o moozæoom
observatory	a csillagvizsgáló	o cheel-logveezhgaalaw
old town	a régi város	o rayghee vaarawsh
opera house	az opera	oz awpæro
palace	a palota	o pollawto
park	a park	o pork
parliament building	a Parlament épülete	o porlommænt aypewlætæ
planetarium	a planetárium	o plonnætaareeoom
port	a kikötő	o keekurtūr
post office	a postahivatal	o pawshtoheevottol
ruins	a romok	o rawmawk
shopping centre	a bevásárló központ	o bævaashaarlaw kurzpawnt
stadium	a stadion	o shtoddeeawn
statue	a szobor	o sawbawr
synagogue	a zsinagóga	o zheenoggawgo
theatre	a színház	o seenhaaz
tomb	a síremlék	o sheeræmlayk
tower	a torony	o tawrawn^y
TV studios	a TV studio	o tayvay shtoodeeaw
university	az egyetem	oz æd^yætæm
zoo	az állatkert	oz aal-lotkært

SZABAD BELÉPÉS   ADMISSION FREE
TILOS A FÉNYKÉPEZÉS   NO CAMERAS ALLOWED

SIGHTSEEING

Admission

Is ... open on Sundays?	A ... vasárnaponként nyitva van?	o ... voshaarnoppawnkaynt n^yeetvo von
When does it open/ close?	Mikor nyit/zár?	meekawr n^yeet/zaar
How much is the entrance fee?	Mennyibe kerül a belépőjegy?	mæn^yeebæ kærewl o bælaypūryæd^y
Is there any reduction for ...?	... részére kedvez- ményes a belépő- jegy?	... rayssayræ kædvæz- mayn^yæsh o bælaypūryæd^y
children	Gyerekek	d^yærækæk
families	Családok	chollaadawk
the handicapped	Nyomorékok	n^yawmawraykawk
pensioners	Nyugdíjasok	n^yoogdēēyoshawk
students	Diákok	deeaakawk
Where can I get a ticket?	Hol lehet jegyet kapni?	hawl læhæt yæd^yæt kopnee
Can I buy a catalogue?	Kaphatok egy katalógust?	kophottawk æd^y kottollāw- goosht
Have you any guide books in English?	Van angolnyelvű útikalauzuk?	von ongawln^yælvēw ōōteekollo-oozook
Is it all right to take pictures?	Szabad fényképezni?	sobbod fayn^ykaypæznee

Who—What—When?

What's that building?	Az az épület mi?	oz oz aypewlæt mee
Who was the ...?	Ki volt ...?	kee vawlt
architect	az építész	oz aypēētayss
artist	a művész	o mēwvayss
painter	a festő	o fæshtūr
sculptor	a szobrász	o sawbraass
Who built it?	Ki építette?	kee aypēētæt-tæ
When was it built?	Mikor épült?	meekawr aypewlt
Who painted this picture?	Ki festette ezt a képet?	kee fæshtæt-tæ æst o kaypæt
When did he live?	Mikor élt?	meekawr aylt
Where's the house in which ... lived?	Hol az a ház, amelyben ... élt?	hawl oz o haaz ommæ^ybæn ... aylt

Just the adjective you've been looking for ...

It's ...   **Ez** ...   æz

awful	**borzasztó**	bawrzostaw
beautiful	**gyönyörű**	dᵛurnᵛurrēw
fantastic	**csodálatos**	chawdaalottawsh
gloomy	**borongós**	bawrawngāwsh
horrible	**rettenetes**	ræt-tænætæsh
impressive	**benyomást keltő**	bænᵛawmaasht kæltūr
interesting	**érdekes**	ayrdækæsh
magnificent	**pompás**	pawmpaash
monumental	**óriási**	āwreeaashee
overwhelming	**lenyűgöző**	lænᵛēwgurzūr
sinister	**rosszhangulatú**	rawshongoolottōō
strange	**különös**	kewlurnursh
superb	**kiváló**	keevaalāw
surprising	**meglepő**	mæglæpūr
ugly	**csúnya**	chōōnᵛo

What's your special interest?

I'm interested in ...   **Bennünket ...**   bæn-newnkæt ... ayr-
                               érdekel/   dækæl/**ayrdækælnæk**
                               érdekelnek.*

antiques	**a régiségek**	o raygheeshaygæk
archaeology	**az archeológia**	oz orhæawlāwgheeo
botany	**a növénytan**	o nurvaynᵛton
coins	**az érmék**	oz ayrmayk
fine arts	**a szépművészet**	o saypmēwvayssæt
furniture	**a bútorok**	o bōōtawrawk
geography	**a földrajz**	o furldroyz
geology	**a földtan**	o furldton
handicrafts	**a mesterségek**	o mæshtærshaygæk
history	**a történelem**	o turrtaynælæm
horticulture	**a kertészet**	o kærtayssæt
Hungarian literature	**a magyar irodalom**	o modᵛor eerawdollawm
languages	**a nyelvek**	o nᵛælvæk
medicine	**az orvostudomány**	oz awrvawshtoodawmaanᵛ
music	**a zene**	o zænæ
natural history	**a természettudo- mányok**	o tærmayssæt-toodaw- maanᵛawk
ornithology	**a madártan**	o moddaarton

---

* Use *érdekelnek* with words in the following list which end in **k**.

painting	a művészetek	o mēwvayssætæk
philately	a bélyeggyüjtés	o bayᵛægdᵛewᵛtaysh
pottery	a fazekasság	o fozzækosh-shaag
prehistory	a történelem előtti kor	o turrtaynælæm ælūrt-tee kawr
science	a tudományok	o toodawmaanᵛawk
sculpture	a szobrászat	o sawbraassot
zoology	az állatvilág	oz aal-lotveelaag
Where's the ... department?	Hol van a/az ...-i részleg?	hawl von o/oz ...-ee rayslæg

Religious services

Over 80 per cent of all Hungarians are Roman Catholics. Minorities include, notably, Protestants and members of the Eastern Orthodox church, and Jews.

Most churches are open to the public. If you visit a church for sightseeing purposes while a service is progress, stay in the rear part of the building so as not to disturb the worshippers. Mass may be said in either Hungarian or Latin.

If you are interested in taking photographs, don't forget to ask permission first.

Is there a ... near here?	Van a közelben ...?	von o kurzælbæn
Catholic church	katolikus templom	kottawleekoosh tæmplawm
mosque	mecset	mæchæt
Protestant church	protestáns templom	prawtæshtaansh tæmplawm
synagogue	zsinagóga	zheenoggāwgo
At what time is ...?	Mikor van ...?	meekawr von
mass	a mise	o meeshæ
the service	a szertartás	o særtortaash
Where can I find a ... who speaks English?	Hol találok egy angolul beszélő ...?	hawl tollaalawk ædᵛ ongawlool bæsaylūr
minister	plébánost	playbaanawsht
priest	papot	poppawt
rabbi	rabit	robbeet

Relaxing

Cinema (movies)—Theatre

A visit to a Hungarian cinema will no doubt be quite an experience, as most foreign films are dubbed into the language of the country. You can expect a newsreel, perhaps a children's cartoon film and a feature film in addition to the main attraction. You'll find out what's showing from local newspapers and a special weekly movie magazine.

Cinemas are open every day of the week. Screening starts as early as 9 a.m., and some cinemas have late-night shows at about midnight.

Since showings are not continuous, you can purchase your ticket up to three days in advance for a specific time. Prices are very reasonable.

Theatre programmes and concerts generally start at 7 p.m. Theatres often close on Mondays.

Tickets can be purchased on the spot, but for a special event you would be wise to make your booking in advance, possibly through a ticket office in the centre of town or a tourist office. Theatre and concert tickets are also very advantageous, even for the National Opera House.

During summer, open-air performances are staged on Margaret Island *Margitsziget* in Budapest. At the same time of year Szeged, in the south of the country, is the scene of a music and opera festival, *Szegedi Ünnepi Játékok.*

Do you have an entertainment guide for ...?	**Van ...-i programjuk?**	von ...-ee **prawgromyook**
What's on at the cinema tonight?	**Mi megy ma este a moziban?**	mee mæd^y mo æshtæ o **mawzeebon**
What's on at the ... Theatre?	**Mit játszanak a ... színházban?**	meet **yaat**sonnok o ... **sēēn**haazbon

What sort of play is it?	**Ez milyen darab?**	æz mee^yæn dorrob
Who is it by?	**Ki a szerző?**	kee o særzūr
Where is …'s new film showing?	**… új filmjét hol játszák?**	… ōō^y feelmyayt hawl yaatsaak
Can you recommend a …?	**Ajánlana egy …?**	oyaanlonno æd^y
cartoon film	**rajzfilmet**	royzfeelmæt
comedy	**bohózatot**	bawhāwzottawt
documentary film	**dokumentum filmet**	dawkoomæntoom feelmæt
good film	**jó filmet**	yāw feelmæt
musical	**zenés színdarabot**	zænaysh sēēndorrobbawt
play	**darabot**	dorrobbawt
revue	**revüt**	rævewt
something light	**valami könnyűt**	vollommee kurn^yēwt
thriller (film)	**bűnügyi filmet**	bēwnewd^yee feelmæt
thriller (play)	**bűnügyi darabot**	bēwnewd^yee dorrobbawt
Western	**vadnyugati filmet**	vodn^yoogottee feelmæt
At which theatre is that new play by … being performed?	**… új darabját hol adják?**	… ōō^y dorrobyaat hawl odyaak
Who's in it?	**Ki játszik benne?**	kee yaatseek bæn-næ
Who's playing the lead?	**Ki játsza a főszerepet?**	kee yaatso o fūrsæræpæt
What time does the show begin?	**Mikor kezdődik a darab?**	meekawr kæzdūrdeek o dorrob
What time does it end?	**Mikor van vége?**	meekawr von vaygæ
Are there any tickets left for tonight?	**Van még jegyük ma estére?**	von mayg yæd^yewk mo æshtayræ
How much are the tickets?	**Mibe kerülnek a jegyek?**	meebæ kærewlnæk o yæd^yæk
I'd like to book 2 seats for next (Friday) evening.	**(Péntek) estére szeretnék 2 jegyet rendelni.**	(payntæk) æshtayræ særætnayk 2 yæd^yæt rændælnee
Can I have a ticket for the matinée on (Tuesday)?	**Kaphatok egy jegyet a (keddi) matinéra?**	kophottawk æd^y yæd^yæt o (kæd-dee) motteenayro
I'd like a seat in the stalls (orchestra)/ circle (mezzanine).	**A földszintre/ Az erkélyre kérek egy jegyet.**	o furldseentræ/ oz ærkay^yræ kayræk æd^y yæd^yæt

How much are the seats in the front row?	**Mibe kerül a jegy az első sorban?**	meebæ kærewl o yæd^y oz ælshūr shawrbon
I want 2 seats in the stalls (orchestra).	**A földszintre kérek 2 jegyet.**	o furldseentræ kayræk 2 yæd^yæt
Somewhere in the middle.	**Valahova középre.**	vollohawvo kurzaypræ
May I have a programme, please?	**Kaphatok egy műsort?**	kophottawk æd^y mēw-shawrt
Where's the cloak-room?	**Hol a ruhatár?**	hawl o roohawtaar

Sajnálom, minden jegyünk elkelt.	I'm sorry, we're sold out.
Csak az erkélyre van még néhány jegyünk.	There are only a few seats left in the circle (mezzanine).
Szabad a jegyét?	May I see your ticket?
Ez az Ön helye.	This is your seat.

Concert—Opera—Ballet

Where's the opera house?	**Hol az operaház?**	hawl oz awpærohaaz
Where's the concert hall?	**Hol a hangverseny-terem?**	hawl o **hong**værshæn^y-tæræm
What's on at the opera tonight?	**Mi megy ma az operában?**	mee mæd^y mo oz awpæ-raabon
Who's singing?	**Ki énekel?**	kee aynækæl
Who's dancing?	**Ki táncol?**	kee taantsawl
What time does the programme start?	**Mikor kezdődik a program?**	meekawr kæzdūīdeek o prawgrom
What's the name of the orchestra?	**Melyik zenekar játszik?**	mæ^yeek zænækor yaatseek
What are they playing?	**Mit játszanak?**	meet yaatsonnok
Who's the conductor?	**Ki vezényel?**	kee væzayn^yæl

RELAXING

Nightclub

Budapest has a number of nightclubs, several of them located in the larger hotels. Similar establishments can be found in lesser quantity in other major towns and, during the summer tourist season, along Lake Balaton.

They generally offer floor shows which, though entertaining, are rather more decorous than those found in some other capital cities—there's no striptease, for example. Music can be very good, and may include live jazz. Prices are predictably high.

Apart from light snacks, no meals are served.

Nightclub hours are from about 10 p.m. to 4 or 5 in the morning, six days a week. The closing day varies. Advance reservations are advisable for the select nightclubs in some five-star hotels, but elsewhere you should have no trouble finding a table.

Can you recommend a good nightclub?	Ajánlana egy jó éjszakai mulatót?	oyaanlonno æd^y yaw ay^{y}sokko-ee moolottawt
Is there a floor show?	Műsor van?	mewshawr von
What time does the floor show start?	Mikor kezdődik a műsor?	meekawr kæzdurdeek o mewshawr
Is evening dress necessary?	Alkalmi öltözet szükséges?	olkolmee urlturzæt sewkshaygæsh

And once inside …

A table for 2, please.	Egy asztalt kérek 2 fő részére.	æd^y ostolt kayræk 2 fur rayssayræ
I've booked a table for 4.	4 fő részére foglaltam asztalt.	4 fur rayssayræ fawgloltom ostolt
My name is …	… vagyok.	… vod^{y}awk
I phoned you earlier.	Az előbb telefonáltam Önöknek.	oz ælurb tælæfawnaaltom urnurknæk
We haven't a reservation.	Nincs foglalásunk.	neench fawglollaashoonk

I'd like the drinks card, please.	**Az itallapot kérem.**	oz eetol-loppawt kayræm
We'd like a bottle of ...	**Egy üveg ... kérünk.**	æd^y ewvaeg ... kayrewnk
champagne	**pezsgőt**	pæzhgūrt
red wine	**vörösbort**	vurrurshbawrt
white wine	**fehérbort**	fæhayrbawrt

Dancing

Would you like to dance?	**Van kedve táncolni?**	von kædvæ taantsawlnee
Where can we go dancing?	**Hol lehet táncolni?**	hawl læhæt taantsawlnee
Is there a discotheque in town?	**Van a városban diszkó?**	von o vaarawshbon deeskāw
Is there an entry fee?	**Belépőjegy van?**	bælaypūṛyæd^y von
There's a dance at the ... Hotel.	**A ... Hotelban lehet táncolni.**	o ... hawtælbon læhæt taantsawlnee
May I have this dance?	**Szabad felkérnem egy táncra?**	sobbod fælkayrnæm æd^y taantsro

Do you happen to play ...?

Chess is a big favourite in Hungary. There is hardly a week without a major tournament being held somewhere.

| Do you play chess? | **Sakkozik?** | shok-kawzeek |

bishop	**futó**	footāw
castle (rook)	**bástya**	baasht^yo
king	**király**	keeraa^y
knight	**huszár**	hoossaar
pawn	**gyalog**	d^yollawg
queen	**vezér**	væzayr
Check!	**Sakk!**	shok
Checkmate!	**Matt!**	mot

RELAXING

Do you play draughts (checkers)?	**Játszik francia sakkot?**	yaatseek frontseeo shok-kawt
Do you play cards?	**Kártyázik?**	kaart^{y}aazeek
bridge	**bridzs**	breedzh
canasta	**kanaszta**	konnosto
gin rummy	**römi**	rurmee
poker	**póker**	pāwkær

hearts	**kőr**	kūrr
diamonds	**káró**	kaaraw̄
clubs	**treff**	træf
spades	**pikk**	peek
ace	**ász**	aass
king	**király**	keeraa^y
queen	**felső**	fælshūr
jack (knave)	**alsó**	olshaw̄
joker	**dzsóker**	dzhaw̄kaer

Sports

The Hungarians are a sport-loving nation, and facilities for both watching and playing sports are widely available.

Soccer *(labdarugás)* is without a doubt the top spectator sport. Most towns have at least one team, and except in the height of summer you'll certainly be able to see a match whatever part of the country you happen to be in.

Basketball *(kosárlabda)* comes second in terms of popularity. It is played all year round, all over the country, in various leagues. The country boasts some 40,000 regular players.

Water polo *(vizilabda)* is another big favourite. The national team has won many international prizes. Main centres are the National Sports Pool *(Nemzeti Sportuszoda)* on Margaret Island and the Komjáti Swimming Pool *(Komjáti Uszoda)*, both in Budapest.

Horse racing *(lóverseny)* is widely organized during the season, with several meetings a week. The Budapest racecourse (track) is called *Budapesti ügető*. Bets can be placed at state-run offices (see page 88).

Sailing *(vitorlázás)* is popular on Lake Balaton and Lake Velence. Regattas and races take place on both lakes between May and October.

Table tennis *(asztalitenisz)* claims around 100,000 regular club players throughout the country, and you should not have too much difficulty in gaining access to a club's facilities during your visit.

Fencing *(vívás)* has a good number of adherents in the country. Its practitioners have made their mark in the field of international competition.

The daily sports paper *Népsport* contains details of what's on in the sporting world—including chess—throughout the country. Any local sports fan with some knowledge of English will be delighted to translate for you and help you find what you want.

Is there a football game on anywhere this Saturday?	**Most szombaton lesz valahol futbalmeccs?**	mawsht **sawm**bottawn læs vollohawl **foot**bol mæch
I'd like to see a basketball match.	**Szeretnék megtekinteni egy kosárlabdamérkőzést.**	sæ**ræt**nayk mægtækeentænee æd^y kawshaarlobdomayrkūrzaysht
Who's playing?	**Ki játszik?**	kee **yaat**seek
What's the admission charge?	**Mibe kerül a belépőjegy?**	**mee**bæ **kæ**rewl o bælay**pūr**-yaed^y
Can you get me 2 tickets?	**Szerezne nekem 2 jegyet?**	sæ**ræz**næ **næ**kæm 2 **yæd**^yæt
Where's the Budapest race-course?	**Hol találom a budapesti ügetőpályát?**	hawl **tol**lawlawm o **boo**doppæshtee **ew**gætūrpaa-^yaat
Where are the tennis courts?	**Hol találok teniszpályát?**	hawl **tol**laalawk tænees**paa**^yaat
Can I hire rackets?	**Bérelhetek ütőket?**	**bay**rælhætæk **ew**tūrkæt

Where can I play table tennis?	Hol lehet ping-pongozni?	hawl læhæt **peeng**-pawngawznee
What's the charge per ...?	Mennyi a bérleti díj ... ?	mæn^Yee o bayrlætee dēē^Y
day	naponta	noppawnto
game	játszmánként	yaatsmaankaynt
hour	óránként	āwraankaynt
Is there a swimming pool near here?	Van a környéken uszoda?	von o kurrn^Yaykæn oossawdo
Is it outdoors or indoors?	Nyitott, vagy fedett?	n^Yeetawt vod^Y fædæt
Can one swim in the lake/river?	Szabad úszni a tóban/folyóban?	sobbod ōōsnee o tāwbon/faw^Yāwbon
Is there any good fishing around here?	Hol lehet a környéken jól horgászni?	hawl læhæt o kurrn^Yaykæn yāwl hawrgaasnoo
Do I need a licence?	Kell hozzá engedély?	kæl **hawz**-zaa ængædæy^Y
Where can I get one?	Hol lehet a horgászengedélyt beszerezni?	hawl læhæt o hawrgaass-ængædæy^Yt bæssæræznee

Betting

Betting on horses and soccer matches is legal and widespread. There is also a state lottery *(lottó)* every week.

The government betting authority, *Sportfogadási és Lottó Igazgatóság* maintains offices in most towns through which you can place your bets on horse races and soccer matches. They also sell lottery tickets. Forms for betting on soccer matches, as well as lottery tickets, can also be obtained from tobacconists', larger news-stands and street vendors. Winnings are paid out in local currency, after deduction of a profits tax.

| Where's the nearest betting shop? | Hol a legközelebbi fogadó iroda? | hawl o lægkurzælæb-bee fawgoddāw eerawdo |

On the beach

Landlocked Hungary may not have a sea coastline, but bathing, boating and sailing facilities are numerous along lake shores and river banks. The approximately 260-square-mile (680-square-kilometre) Lake Balaton is a special favourite, and its shallow waters are generally quite safe, provided normal precautions are taken. Note that power boats are not allowed on Balaton, so you'll have to go elsewhere for water-skiing (the Danube, Tisza and other rivers).

Is it safe for swimming?	**Itt biztonságos az úszás?**	eet **beez**tawnshaagawsh oz ōōssaash
Is there a lifeguard?	**Mentőszolgálat van?**	mæntūrsaawlgaalot von
Is it safe for children?	**Gyerekek részére biztonságos?**	d**Y**ærækæk rayssayræ **beez**tawnshaagawsh
The lake is very calm.	**A tó nagyon nyugodt.**	o tāw nod**Y**awn n**Y**oogawdt
Are there any dangerous currents?	**Nincsenek veszélyes örvények?**	neenchænæk væssay**Y**æsh urrvayn**Y**æk

MAGÁN STRAND	TILOS A FÜRDÉS
PRIVATE BEACH	NO BATHING

What's the temperature of the water?	**Mennyi a víz hőmérséklete?**	mæn**Y**ee o vēēz hūr-mayrshayklætæ
I'd like to hire a/an/some...	**Szeretnék bérelni egy ....**	særætnayk bayrælnee æd**Y**
air mattress	**gumimatracot**	goomeemotrotsawt
deck chair	**nyugágyat**	n**Y**oogaad**Y**ot
kayak	**kajakot**	koyokkawt
rowing boat	**evezős csónakot**	ævæzūrsh chāwnokkawt
sailing boat	**vitorláshajót**	veetawrlaashhoyāwt
skin-diving equipment	**búvárfelszerelést**	bōōvaarfælsærælaysht
water skis	**vizisít**	veezeeshēēt
What's the charge per hour?	**Mibe kerül óránként?**	meebæ kærewl āwraankaynt

RELAXING

Camping—Countryside

Camping facilities are available at about 200 sites, the majority of which are clustered around Lake Balaton, South-West of Budapest. They are graded in three categories according to the amenities and services they offer. First- and second-class sites have shops, restaurants, showers, toilets and electrical outlets for campers. Tents and cabins can be rented at first-class sites.

If you wish to have the freedom of camping but a little more comfort, you can rent a holiday home sleeping from two to six people. Here you'll be able to enjoy various extra services including laundry, catering, shopping and some sports facilities. Some units have their own little gardens.

Most camping sites and holiday-home centres operate from May to October.

Foreign visitors generally find rates very advantageous, and members of internationally affiliated camping and caravaning clubs often enjoy reductions. Bills can be paid in local currency.

Lists of camping sites and holiday homes detailing facilities and rates can be obtained from local and foreign branches of Ibusz (see page 28 for addresses abroad), most hotels, the Hungarian Motoring Association *(Magyar Autóklub)* or the Hungarian Camping and Caravaning Club *(Magyar Kemping és Karaván Klub)*.

Is there a camping site near here?	**Van a közelben kemping?**	von o kurzælbæn kæmpeeng
Have you room for a tent/caravan (trailer)?	**Van helyük egy sátor/lakókocsi részére?**	von hæ^yewk æd^y shaa-tawr/lokkāwkawchee ray-ssayræ
Where can we rent a holiday home?	**Hol bérelhetnénk egy nyaralót?**	hawl bayrælhætnaynk æd^y n^yorrollāwt

CAMPING: see also page 106

May we light a fire?	**Szabad tüzet gyújtani?**	sobbod tewzæt d$^Y\overline{oo}^Y$tonnee
Is this drinking water?	**Ivóvíz van?**	eev$\overline{aw}$v$\overline{ee}$z von
Are there any shops on the site?	**Vannak üzletek a kemping területén?**	von-nok ewzlætæk o kæmpeeng tærewlætayn
Are there any ...?	**Vannak ...?**	von-nok
baths	**fürdőszobák**	fewrd$\overline{u}$rssawbaak
kitchens	**konyhák**	kawn^{Y}haak
laundry facilities	**mosódák**	mawsh$\overline{aw}$daak
showers	**zuhanyozók**	zoohon^{Y}awz$\overline{aw}$k
toilets	**vécék**	vaytsayk
What's the charge ...?	**Mennyibe kerül ...?**	mæn^{Y}eebæ kærewl
per day	**naponta**	noppawnto
per person	**személyenként**	sæmay^{Y}ænkaynt
for a car	**gépkocsinként**	gaypkawcheenkaynt
for a tent	**sátranként**	shaatronkaynt
for a caravan	**lakókocsinként**	lokk$\overline{aw}$kawcheenkaynt
Do you known anyone who can put us up for the night?	**Ismer valakit, akinél éjszakára megszállhatunk?**	eeshmær vollokkeet okkeenayl ay^{Y}ssokkaaro mægsaalhottoonk

TÁBOROZNI TILOS	**TILOS LAKÓKOCSIVAL PARKIROZNI**
NO CAMPING	NO CARAVANS (TRAILERS)

Landmarks

barn	**a csűr**	o ch$\overline{ew}$r
beach	**a part**	o port
bridge	**a híd**	o h$\overline{ee}$d
brook	**a patak**	o pottok
building	**az épület**	oz aypewlæt
canal	**a csatorna**	o chottawrno
castle	**a vár**	o vaar
church	**a templom**	o tæmplawm
cliff	**a szikla**	o seeklo
cottage	**a tanya**	o ton^{Y}o
crossroads	**a keresztút**	o kæræst$\overline{oo}$t
farm	**a gazdaság**	o gozdoshaag
ferry	**a komp**	o kawmp
field	**a szántóföld**	o saant$\overline{aw}$furld

forest	az erdő	oz ærdūr
fortress	az erődítmény	oz ærürdēetmayn^y
hamlet	a kunyhó	o koon^yhāw
highway	az országút	oz awrsaagōōt
hill	a domb	o dawmb
house	a ház	o haaz
hut	a menedékház	o mænædayk-haaz
inn	a vendéglő	o vændayglūr
lake	a tó	o tāw
marsh	a mocsaras	o mawchorrosh
moorland	a legelő	o lægælūr
mountain	a hegy	o hæd^y
path	az ösvény	oz urshvayn^y
peak	a csúcs	o chōōch
pond	a tavacska	o tovvochko
pool	a víztároló	o vēēztaarawlāw
railway line	a vasúti pálya	o voshōōtee paa^yo
river	a folyó	o faw^yāw
road	az út	oz ōōt
ruin	a rom	o rawm
spring	a forrás	o fawr-raash
stream	a folyam	o faw^yom
swamp	a mocsár	o mawchaar
tower	a torony	o tawrawn^y
track	a földút	o furldōōt
tree	a fa	o fo
valley	a völgy	o vurld^y
village	a falu	o folloo
vineyard	a szölő	o surlūr
water	a víz	o vēēz
waterfall	a vízesés	o vēēzæshaysh
well	a kút	o kōōt
wood	a liget	o leegæt

| What's the name of that river? | Mi a folyó neve? | mee o faw^yāw nævæ |
| How high is that mountain? | Milyen magas az a hegy? | mee^yæn moggosh oz o hæd^y |

... and if you're tired of walking, you can always try hitch-hiking *(autóstoppal utazni)*:

| Can you give me a lift to ...? | Elvinne ...-ba/-be/ -ra/-re?* | ælveen-næ ...-bo/-bæ/ -ro/-ræ |

---

* See Grammar section for word endings.

Making friends

Introductions

A few phrases to get you started:

How do you do?	Jónapot kívánok.	yāwnoppawt kēēvaanawk
How are you?	Hogy van?	hawd^y von
Fine, thank you. And you?	Jól, köszönöm. És Ön?	yāwl kursurnurm. aysh urn
I'd like you to meet a friend of mine.	Szeretném bemutatni az egyik barátomat.	særætnaym bæmoototnee oz æd^{y}eek borraatawmot
May I introduce ...?	Bemutathatom ...?	bæmootot-hotawm
John, this is ...	John, ez ...	dzhawn æz
My name is ...	A nevem ...	o nævæm
Glad to know you.	Örülök, hogy megismerhetem.	urrewlurk hawd^y mægeeshmærhætæm
... sends his/her best regards.	... szívélyesen üdvözli.	... sēēvayl^{y}æssæn ewdvurzlee
It's nice to see you (again).	Örülök hogy (újra) találkozunk.	urrewlurk hawd^y ($\overline{oo}^y$ro) tollaalkawzoonk

Follow-up

How long have you been here?	Mióta van itt?	meeāwto von eet
We've been here a week.	Egy hete vagyunk itt.	æd^y hætæ vod^{y}oonk eet
Is this your first visit?	Most vannak itt először?	mawsht von-nok eet ælürssurr
No, we came here last year.	Nem, már tavaly is itt voltunk.	næm maar tovvoy eesh eet vawltoonk
Are you enjoying your stay?	Jól érzik magukat?	yāwl ayrzeek moggookot
Yes, I like ... very much.	Igen ... nagyon tetszik.	eegæn ... nod^{y}awn tætseek
I like the country-side a lot.	Nagyon szeretem a vidéket.	nod^{y}awn særætæm o veedaykæt

This is a very interesting town.	Ez nagyon érdekes város.	æz nod^yawn ayrdækæsh vaarawsh
Are you on your own?	Egyedül van?	æd^yædewl von
I'm with ...	... vagyok.	... vod^yawk
my husband	A férjemmel	o fayryæm-mæl
my wife	A feleségemmel	o fælæshaygæm-mæl
my family	A családommal	o chollaadawm-mol
my children	A gyerekeimmel	o d^yæækæeem-mæl
my parents	A szüleimmel	o sewlæeem-mæl
some friends	Néhány barátommal	nayhaan^y borraatawm-mol
Where do you come from?	Honnan jön?	hawn-non yurn
Where are you staying?	Hol lakik?	hawl lokkeek
I'm a student.	Diák vagyok.	deeaak vod^yawk
What are you studying?	Mit tanul?	meet tonnool
I'm here on business.	Hivatalosan vagyok itt.	heevottollawshon vod^yawk eet
What kind of business are you in?	Mi a foglalkozása?	mee o fawglolkawzaasho
I hope we'll meet again.	Remélem, hamarosan.	ræmaylæm hommo-rawshon

The weather

The Hungarians love to talk about it—in fact, they like to blame most things that go wrong on the weather!

What a lovely day!	Gyönyörű napunk van!	d^yurn^yurrēw noppoonk von
What awful weather!	Micsoda pocsék idő van!	meechawdo pawchayk eedūr von
Isn't it cold/hot today!	Nincs hideg/meleg?	neench heedæg/mælæg
Do you think it will ... tomorrow?	Mit gondol, holnap ...?	meet gawndawl hawlnop
clear up	kiderül	keedærewl
rain	esik	æsheek
snow	havazik	hovvozzeek
be sunny	süt a nap	shewt o nop

Invitations

My wife/My husband and I would like you to join us for dinner.	Feleségemmel/Férjemmel együtt szeretnénk ha velünk vacsoráznának.	fælæshaygæm-mæl/fayr-yæm-mæl æd^yewt særætnaynk ho vælewnk vochawraaznaanok
Can you come to dinner tonight?	Eljönne ma este vacsorára?	ælyurn-næ mo æshtæ vochawraaro
Can you come over for a drink this evening?	Átjönne ma este egy italra?	aatyurn-næ mo æshtæ æd^y eetolro
There's a party. Are you coming?	Összejövetelünk van. Eljön?	urs-sæ^yurvætælewnk von. ælyurn
That's very kind of you.	Nagyon kedves Öntől.	nod^yawn kædvæsh urn-türl
Great! I'd love to come.	Nagyszerű. Szívesen eljönnék.	nod^ysærēw. sēēvæshæn ælyurn-nayk
What time shall we come?	Mikor jöjjünk?	meekawr yur^y-yewnk
May I bring a friend/ girl friend?	Egy barátomat/ barátnőmet is elhozhatom?	æd^y borraatawmot/ borraatnūrmæt eesh ælhawz-hottawm
I'm afraid we've got to go now.	Azt hiszem, most már mennünk kell.	ost heessæm mawsht maar mæn-newnk kæl
Next time, you must come to visit us.	Legközelebb feltétlenül látogassanak meg.	lægkurzælæb fæltaytlænewl laatawgosh-shonnok mæg
Thanks for the evening.	Köszönet az estéért.	kursurnæt oz æshtayayrt
I/We enjoyed it very much.	Nagyon élveztem/ élveztünk.	nod^yawn aylvæztæm/ aylvæztewnk

Dating

May I get you a drink?	Meghívhatom egy italra?	mæghēēvhottawm æd^y eetolro
Would you like a cigarette?	Parancsol egy cigarettát?	porronchawl æd^y tseegorræt-taat
Excuse me, could you give me a light?	Bocsánat, van tüze?	bawchaanot von tewzæ

Are you waiting for someone?	**Vár valakire?**	vaar vollokkeeræ
Leave me alone, please!	**Kérem, hagyjon békén!**	kayræm hod^Yawn baykayn
Are you free this evening?	**Ráérne ma este?**	raaayrnæ mo æshtæ
I'm sorry, I already have an engagement this evening.	**Sajnálom, de ma estére már van programom.**	shoynaalawm dæ mo æshtayræ maar von prawgrommawm
Would you like to go out with me tomorrow night?	**Eljönne velem holnap este?**	ælyurn-næ vælæm hawlnop æshtæ
Would you like to go dancing?	**Lenne kedve táncolni?**	læn-næ kædvæ taantsawlnee
I know a good discotheque.	**Tudok egy jó diszkót.**	toodawk æd^Y yāw dees-kāwt
Do you know a good discotheque?	**Ismer egy jó diszkót?**	eeshmær æd^Y yāw dees-kāwt
Shall we go to the cinema?	**Menjünk moziba?**	mæn^Yewnk mawzeebo
Would you like to go for a drive?	**Van kedve autózni egyet?**	von kædvæ ooootāwznee æd^Yæt
Where shall we meet?	**Hol találkozzunk?**	hawl tollaalkawz-zoonk
I'll pick you up at your hotel.	**A szállodájánál majd felveszem.**	o saal-lawdaa^Yaanaal moyd fælvæsæm
I'll call for you at 8.	**8 órakor magáért jövök.**	8 āwrok-kawr moggaa-ayrt yurvurk
May I take you home?	**Hazakisérhetem?**	hozzokkeeshayrhætæm
Can I see you again tomorrow?	**Holnap újra láthatom?**	hawlnop ōō^Yro laat-hottawm
Thank you, it's been a very enjoyable evening.	**Köszönöm. Nagyon szép este volt.**	kursurnurm. nod^Yawn sayp æshtæ vawlt
What's your telephone number?	**Mi a telefonszáma?**	mee o tælæfawnsaamo
What time is your last bus/train?	**Mikor indul az utolsó autóbusza/ villamosa?**	meekawr eendool oz oo-tawlshāw ooootāwboosso/ veel-lommawsho

Shopping guide

This shopping guide is designed to help you find what you want with ease, accuracy and speed. It features:

1. a list of all major shops, stores and services (p. 98)
2. some general expressions required when shopping to allow you to be selective and specific (p. 100)
3. full details of the shops and services most likely to concern you. Here you'll find advice, alphabetical lists of items and conversion charts, as listed under the headings below.

		Page
Bookshop	books, newspapers, magazines, stationery	104
Camping	camping equipment	106
Chemist's (drugstore)	medicines, first-aid supplies, cosmetics, toilet articles	108
Clothing	clothes, shoes, accessories	112
Electrical appliances	radios, tape-recorders, records, shavers, batteries, etc.	119
Hairdresser	men's and ladies' hairdressers', beauty salon	121
Jeweller— Watch shop	jewellery, watches, watch repairs	123
Laundry—Dry cleaning	usual facilities	126
Photography	cameras, accessories, film, developing	127
Provisions	this section is confined to basic items required for picnics	129
Souvenirs	souvenirs, gifts, fancy goods, local specialities	131
Tobacconist	smokers' supplies	132

SHOPPING GUIDE

Shops—Stores—Services

Most shops are open from 10 a.m. to 6 p.m. (department stores from 9 a.m. to 7 p.m.), Monday–Friday, and from 9 a.m. to 2 p.m., Saturday, without a break. Some tobacconists' and most pastry shops also stay open on Sunday. Grocers' and dairy shops may start as early as 6 a.m.

Price tags in Hungarian shops show the price you actually pay. No tax is added, and discounts are not negotiable.

Intertourist shops, found in most main centres, are likely to have a wider range of goods on sale than you'll see elsewhere. Payment must be made in hard currency. Imported items such as whisky, perfumes, cigarettes and appliances will often be less expensive in these shops than at home.

Where's the nearest ...?	Hol van a legközelebbi ...?	hawl von o lægkurzælæb-bæ
antique shop	régiség-kereskedés	raygheeshayg-kæræshkædaysh
art gallery	képzőművészeti galéria	kaypzūrmēwvaysætee gollayreeo
baker	pék	payk
barber	borbély	bawrbay^V
beauty salon	kozmetikai szalon	kawzmæteeko-ee sollawn
bookshop	könyvesbolt	kurn^{V}væshbawlt
butcher	hentes	hæntæsh
camera shop	fotószaküzlet	fawtāwsokkewzlæt
candy store	édességbolt	aydæsh-shaygbawlt
chemist	gyógyszertár	d^{V}āwd^{V}særtaar
confectioner	cukrászda	tsookraasdo
dairy shop	tejbolt	tæ^{V}bawlt
delicatessen	csemegebolt	chæmægæbawlt
department store	áruház	aaroohaaz
drugstore	illatszerbolt	eel-lotsærbawlt
dry-cleaner	vegytisztító	væd^{V}teestēētāw
fishmonger	halkereskedés	holkæræshkædaysh
florist	virágüzlet	veeraaghewzlæt
furrier	szőrme üzlet	sūrrmæ ewzlæt
greengrocer	zöldségesbolt	zurldshaygæshbawlt
grocer	élelmiszerbolt	aylælmeessærbawlt
hairdresser (ladies')	női-fodrászat	nūr-ee-fawdraassot
hairdresser (men's)	férfi-fodrászat	fayrfee-fawdraassot

hardware store	vasüzlet	voshewzlæt
Intertourist shop	**Intertourist bolt**	"intertourist" bawlt
jeweller	ékszerész	ayksærayss
laundry	mosoda	mawshawdo
liquor store	szeszes italok	sæsæsh eetollawk
market	piac	peeots
newstand	újságárus	$\overline{oo}$Yshaagaaroosh
off-licence	szeszes italok	sæsæsh eetollawk
optician	látszerész	laatsærayss
pastry shop	cukrászda	tsookraasdo
pharmacy	gyógyszertár	dY$\overline{awd}$Ysærtaar
photo shop	fotószaküzlet	fawt$\overline{aw}$sokkewzlæt
shoemaker (repairs)	cipőjavító	tseepūr-yov$\overline{ee}$t$\overline{aw}$
shoe shop	cipőbolt	tseepūrbawlt
souvenir shop	szuvenírbolt	soovæn$\overline{ee}$rbawlt
sports shop	sportszerkeres-kedés	shpawrtsærkæræshkæ-daysh
stationer	papírüzlet	popp$\overline{ee}$rewzlæt
supermarket	szupermarket	soopærmaarkæt
sweet shop	édességbolt	aydæsh-shaygbawlt
tailor	szabó	sobb$\overline{aw}$
tobacconist	dohánybolt	dawhaanYbawlt
toy shop	játéküzlet	yaataykewzlæt
travel agency	utazási iroda	ootozzaashee eerawdo
vegetable store	zöldségbolt	zurldshaygbawlt
watchmaker	órás	$\overline{aw}$raash
wine merchant	bor szaküzlet	bawr sokkewzlæt

SHOPPING GUIDE

...and some other useful addresses:

bank	**bank**	bonk
currency exchange office	valuta beváltó hely	vollooto bævaalt$\overline{aw}$ hæY
dentist	fogorvos	fawgawrvawsh
doctor	orvos	awrvawsh
filling station	töltőállomás	turlt$\overline{u}$raal-lawmaash
hospital	kórház	k$\overline{aw}$rhaaz
library	könyvtár	kurnYvtaar
lost property (lost-and found) office	talált tárgyak hivatala	tollaalt taardYok heevotollo
police station	rendőrség	rænd$\overline{u}$rshayg
post office	posta	pawshto
telegraph office	távirda	taaveerdo
tourist office	turista ügynökség	tooreeshto ewdYnurk-shayg

Where?

Where's there a good ...?	**Hol van egy jó ...?**	hawl von æd^y yaw
Where can I find a ...?	**Hol találok egy ...?**	hawl tollaalawk æd^y
Where can I buy ...?	**Hol kapok ...?**	hawl koppawk
Can you recommend an inexpensive ...?	**Ajánlana egy olcsó ...?**	oyaanlonno æd^y awlchaw
Where's the main shopping area?	**Hol a bevásárlóközpont?**	hawl o bævaashaarlaw-kurzpawnt
Is it far from here?	**Messze van innen?**	mæs-sæ von een-næn
How do I get there?	**Hogy jutok el oda?**	hawd^y yootawk æl awdo
Where's the courtesy desk?	**Hol a vevőszolgálat?**	hawl o vævūrsawlgaalot

Service

Can you help me?	**Segítene?**	shægeetænæ
I'm just looking round.	**Csak nézelődök.**	chok nayzælūrdurk
I want ...	**Szükségem van egy ...**	sewkshaygæm von æd^y
Can you show me some ...?	**Mutatna néhány ...?**	moototno nayhaan^y
Do you have any ...?	**Kapható ...?**	kophottaw

That one

Can you show me ...?	**Láthatnám ...?**	laathotnaam
that one	**azt**	ost
those	**azokat**	ozzawkot
the one in the window	**azt ott a kirakatban.**	ost awt o keerokkotbon
It's over there.	**Ott van.**	awt von

| KIÁRUSÍTÁS | VÉGKIÁRUSÍTÁS |
| SALE | CLEARANCE |

Defining the article

I'd like a … one.	**…-ra/-re van szükségem.***	… -ro/-ræ von **sewk**shaygæm
It must be …	**…-ra/-re gondolok.***	… -ro/-ræ **gawn**dawlawk

big	**nagy**	nod^y
cheap	**olcsó**	awlchāw
dark	**sötét**	shurtayt
good	**jó**	yāw
heavy	**nehéz**	næhayz
large	**nagy**	nod^y
light (colour)	**világos**	veelaagawsh
light (weight)	**könnyű**	kurn^yēw
oval	**ovális**	awvaaleesh
rectangular	**négyzetes**	nayd^yzætæsh
round	**kerek**	kæræk
small	**kicsi**	keechee
soft	**puha**	pooho
square	**négyszögű**	nayd^ysurgēw

I don't want anything too expensive.	**Nem valami drága holmira gondolok.**	næm **voll**ommee draago hawlmeero **gawn**dawlawk

Preference

Haven't you anything …?	**Nincs valami …?**	neench **voll**ommee
better/cheaper	**jobb/olcsóbb**	yawb/**awl**chāwb
larger/smaller	**nagyobb/kisebb**	nod^yawb/**kee**shæb
Can you show me some more?	**Mutatna még másfélét is?**	moototno mayg **maash**faylayt eesh

How much?

How much is this?	**Mibe kerül?**	meebæ kærewl
Please write it down.	**Kérem, írja le.**	kayræm **ēē**ryo læ
I don't want to spend more than …	**Nem akarok többet mint …-t költeni.**	næm okkorrawk **turb**-bæt meent …-t **kurl**tænee

*See Grammar section for word endings.

Decision

| I'll take it. | **Ezt megveszem.** | æst **m**ægvæsæm |
| No, I don't like it. | **Nem, nem tetszik.** | næm næm **t**ætseek |

Ordering

Can you order it for me?	**Megrendelné a részemre?**	**m**ægrændælnay o **ray**-sæmræ
How long will it take?	**Meddig kell várni?**	mæd-deeg kæl **vaar**nee
I'd like it as soon as possible.	**A lehető leggyorsabban szeretném megkapni.**	o læhætūr lægd^yawr-shob-bon særætnaym mægkopnee

Delivery

Please deliver it to the ... Hotel.	**Kérem, szállítsa le a ... szállodába!**	kayræm **saal**-lēētsho læ o ... **saal**-lawdaabo
Please send it to this address.	**Kérem, küldje el erre a címre!**	kayræm **kewl**d^yæ æl ær-ræ o **tsēē**mræ
Will I have any difficulty with the customs?	**Nem lesz problémám a vámnál?**	næm læs **prawb**laymaam o **vaam**naal

Paying

How much is it?	**Mibe kerül?**	**mee**bæ **kæ**rewl
Can I pay with traveller's cheques?	**Fizethetek traveller's csekkel?**	**fee**zæt-hætæk **tro**vvæl-lærs **chæk**-kæl
Do you accept credit cards?	**Hitelkártyát elfogadnak?**	**hee**tælkaart^yat æl-**faw**godnok
Do you accept ... ?	**Elfogadnak ... ?**	**æl**fawgodnok
U.S. dollars	**amerikai dollárt**	om**mæ**reeko-ee **dawl**-laart
Canadian dollars	**kanadai dollárt**	**kon**noddo-ee **dawl**-laart
pounds sterling	**angol fontot**	**on**gawl **fawn**tawt
Can I please have a receipt?	**Kaphatok egy elismervényt?**	**kop**hottawk æd^y **æ**leesh-mærvayn^yt
Haven't you made a mistake in the bill?	**Nem állította tévesen össze a számlát?**	næm **aal**-lēētawt-to **tay**væ-shæn **urs**-sæ o **saam**laat
Will you please wrap it?	**Becsomagolva kéri?**	**bæ**chawmoggawlvo **kay**ree

CHANGING MONEY: see page 135

Anything else?

No thanks, that's all.	**Nem, köszönöm. Ez minden.**	næm **kur**surnurm. æz **meen**dæn
Yes, please show me ...	**Igen, kérem mutassa meg nekem a ...**	**ee**gæn **kay**ræm **moo**tosh-sho mæg **næk**æm o
Could I have a carrier bag, please?	**Kérnék egy szatyrot.**	**kayr**nayk æd^y **sot**^yrawt
Thank you.	**Köszönöm.**	**kur**surnurm
Goodbye.	**Viszontlátásra.**	**vee**ssawntlaataashro

Segíthetek ...?	Can I help you?
Mit parancsol?	What are you looking for?
Milyen ... parancsol?	What ... would you like?
színt/fazont	colour/shape
minőséget/mennyiséget	quality/quantity
Sajnálom, ilyent nem tartunk.	I'm sorry, we haven't any.
Elfogyott.	We're out of stock.
Megrendeljük az Ön részére?	Shall we order it for you?
Összesen ... forintba kerül kérem.	That's ... forints, please.
A pénztár ott van.	You pay over there.
Hitelkártyát/Traveller's csekket nem fogadunk el.	We don't accept credit cards/ traveller's cheques.

SHOPPING GUIDE

Dissatisfied

Can you please exchange this?	**Kicserélné ezt?**	**kee**chæraylnay æst
I want to return this.	**Ezt vissza akarom váltani.**	æst **vees**-so **ok**korrawm **vaal**tonnee
I'd like a refund.	**Kérem a vételár visszatérítését.**	**kay**ræm o **vay**tælaar **vees**-sottayrēētayshayt
Here's the receipt.	**Itt az elismervény.**	eet oz æleeshmærvayn^y

Bookshop—Stationer's—Newsstand

In Hungary, books and stationery items are usually sold in separate shops. Newspapers and magazines are sold at newsstands and at post offices. Western dailies and news-magazines are only available at major hotels. Some book-shops also sell records (see page 120 for useful phrases).

(see page 120 for useful phrases)

Where's the nearest ...?	Hol a legközelebbi ...?	hawl o lægkurzælæb-bee
bookshop	könyvesbolt	kurn^yvæshbawlt
newsstand	újságáruda	ōō^yshaagaaroodo
stationer's	papír és írószer-kereskedés	poppēēr aysh ēērāwssær-kæræshkædaysh
Where can I buy an English-language newspaper?	Hol kapok angol-nyelvű újságot?	hawl koppawk ongawl-n^yælvēw ōō^yshaagawt
I'd like a/an/some ...	Kérnék ...	kayrnayk
address book	egy címregisztert	aed^y tsēēmrægheestært
ballpoint pen	egy golyóstollat	æd^y gaw^yāwshtawl-lot
book	egy könyvet	æd^y kurn^yvæt
box of paints	egy doboz festéket	æd^y dawbawz fæshtaykæt
carbon paper	másolópapírt	maashawlāwpoppēērt
cellophane tape	ragasztó szalagot	roggostāw solloggawt
crayons	krétát	kraytaat
dictionary	egy szótárt	æd^y sāwtaart
English-Hungarian	angol-magyar	ongawl-mod^Vor
pocket dictionary	zsebszótárt	zhæbsāwtaart
drawing paper	rajzpapírt	royzpoppēērt
drawing pins	rajzszeget	royzsægæt
envelopes	néhány borítékot	nayhaan^y bawrēētaykawt
eraser	radírt	roddēērt
exercise book	egy füzetet	æd^y fewzætæt
fountain pen	egy töltőtollat	æd^y turltūrtawl-lot
glue	ragasztót	roggostāwt
grammar book	egy tankönyvet	æd^y tonkurn^Vvæt
guide book	egy útikalauzt	æd^y ooteekollo-oozt
ink	tintát	teentaat
black/blue/red	fekete/kék/piros	fækætæ/kayk/peerawsh
magazine	egy képes folyóiratot	æd^y kaypæsh faw^yāweerottawt
map	egy térképet	æd^y tayrkaypæt
of the town	egy várostérképet	æd^y vaarawshtayrkaypæt
road map	egy térképet	æd^y tayrkaypæt

SHOPPING GUIDE

newspaper	egy ... újságot	æd^y ... $\overline{oo}^y$shaagawt
American	amerikai	ommæreeko-ee
English	angol	ongawı
notebook	egy jegyzetfüzetet	æd^y yæd^{y}zætfewzætæt
note paper	jegyzetpapírt	yæd^{y}zætpoppēērt
paperback	egy zsebkönyvet	æd^y zhæbkurn^{y}væt
paper napkins	csomagolópapírt	chawmoggāwlawpoppēērt
paste	ragasztót	roggostāwt
pen	egy tollat	æd^y tawl-lot
pencil	egy ceruzát	æd^y tsæroozaat
pencil sharpener	egy ceruza-hegyezőt	æd^y tsæroozohæd^{y}æzūrt
picture book	egy képeskönyvet	æd^y kaypæshkurn^{y}væt
playing cards	kártyát	kaart^{y}aat
postcards	levelező-lapokat	lævælæzūr-loppawkot
rubber	radírt	roddēērt
ruler	egy vonalzót	æd^y vawnolzāwt
sketchpad	egy vázlatfüzetet	æd^y vaazlotfewzætæt
string	zsineget	zheenægæt
thumbtacks	rajzszeget	royzsægæt
tissue paper	selyempapírt	shæ^{y}æmpoppēērt
typewriter ribbon	írógépszalagot	ēērāwgaypsolloggawt
typing paper	gépíró-papírt	gaypēērāw-poppēērt
wrapping paper	papír szalvétákat	poppēēr solvaytaakot
writing pad	egy jegyzettömböt	æd^y yæd^{y}zæt-turmburt
Where's the guide-book section?	Hol találom az útikalauzrészleget?	hawl tollaalawm oz ooteekollo-oozrayslægæt
Where do you keep the English books?	Hol tartják az angolnyelvű köny-veket?	hawl tort^{y}aak oz ongawl-n^{y}ælvēw kurn^{y}vækæt
Have you any of ...'s books in English?	Angol nyelven megvan ... valamelyik műve?	ongawl n^{y}ælvæn mæg-von ... vollommæ^{y}eek mēwvæ

SHOPPING GUIDE

Here are some Hungarian authors whose books are available in English translation. In accordance with Hungarian usage, we have given the writer's surname first.

Arany János
Jókai Mór
József Attila

Mikszáth Kálmán
Petőfi Sándor
Rejtő Jenő*

---

*In English translation, Rejto's works are published under the name P. Howard.

Camping

Here we're concerned with items of equipment you may need.

I'd like a/an/some ...	Szeretnék ...	sæerætnayk
bottle opener	egy üvegnyítót	æd^y ewvaegn^yēētāwt
bucket	egy vödröt	æd^y vurdrurt
camp bed	egy tábori ágyat	æd^y taabawree aad^yot
can opener	egy konzervnyitót	æd^y kawnzærn^yeetāwt
candles	gyertyákat	d^yært^yaakot
chair	egy széket	æd^y saykæt
folding chair	egy összecsukható széket	æd^y urs-sæchook-hottāw saykæt
clothes-pegs	ruhaakasztó csipeszeket	rooho-okkostāw cheepæsækæt
corkscrew	egy dugóhúzót	æd^y doogāwhōōzāwt
crockery	edényeket	ædayn^yækæt
cutlery	evőeszközöket	ævūræskurzurkæt
deck chair	egy nyugágyat	æd^y n^yoogaad^yot
first-aid kit	egy elsősegély-dobozt	æd^y ælshűrshægay^y-dawbawzt
fishing tackle	egy horgász-felszerelést	æd^y hawrgaasfælsæræ-laysht
flashlight	egy zseblámpát	æd^y zhæblaampaat
frying pan	egy tepsit	æd^y tæpsheet
groundsheet	egy pokrócot	æd^y pawkrāwtsawt
hammer	egy kalapácsot	æd^y kolloppaachawt
hammock	egy függőágyat	æd^y fewg-gūraad^yot
ice-bag	egy hütőtáskát	æd^y hewtūrtaashkaat
kerosene	petróleumot	pætrāwlæoomawt
kettle	egy fazekat	æd^y fozzækot
lamp	lámpát	laampaat
lantern	egy lámpást	æd^y laampaasht
matches	gyufát	d^yoofaat
mattress	egy matracot	æd^y motrotsawt
air mattress	egy gumimatracot	æd^y goomeemotrotsawt
methylated spirits	főzőspirituszt	fūrzūrshpeereetoost
nails	szeget	sægæt
pail	egy vödröt	æd^y vurdrurt
paraffin	petróleumot	pætrāwlæoomawt
penknife	egy zsebkést	æd^y zhæbkaysht
picnic case	egy kiránduló táskát	æd^y keeraandoolāw taashkaat
plastic bags	nájlonszatyrot	næ^ylawnsot^yrawt

CAMPING: see also page 90

SHOPPING GUIDE

pot	egy fazekat	æd^y fozzækot
pressure cooker	egy kuktát	æd^y kooktaat
rope	kötelet	kurtælæt
rucksack	egy hátizsákot	æd^y haateezhaakawt
saucepan	egy nyeles serpenyőt	æd^y n^yælæsh shær-pæn^yūrt
scissors	egy ollót	æd^y awl-lāwt
screwdriver	egy dugóhúzót	æd^y doogāwhōōzāwt
sheath knife	egy tőrt	æd^y tūrrt
sleeping bag	egy hálózsákot	æd^y haalāwzhaakawt
stewpan	egy serpenyőt	æd^y shærpæn^yūrt
stove	egy kályhát	æd^y kaa^yhaat
string	zsineget	zheenægæt
table	egy asztalt	æd^y ostolt
folding table	egy összecsukható asztalt	æd^y urs-sæchook-hottāw ostolt
tent	egy sátrat	æd^y shaatrot
tent pegs	sátorcölöpöket	shaatawrtsurlurpurkæt
tent pole	egy sátorrudat	æd^y shaatawr-roodot
tin opener	egy konzervnyitót	æd^y kawnzærvn^yeetāwt
tongs	egy fogót/egy csipeszt	æd^y fawgāwt/æd^y chee-pæst
tool kit	egy szerszámosládát	æd^y særsaamawshlaadaat
torch	egy zseblámpát	æd^y zhæblaampaat
vacuum flask (bottle)	egy hőpalackot	æd^y hūrpollotskawt
water carrier	egy vizhordót	æd^y veezhawrdāwt
wood alcohol	faszeszt	fossæst

Crockery

cups	csészék	chayssayk
mugs	bögrék	burgrayk
plates	tányérok	taan^yayrawk
saucers	csészealjak	chayssæolyok

Cutlery

forks	villák	veel-laak
knives	kések	kayshæk
spoons	kanalak	konnollok
teaspoons	teáskanalak	tæaashkonnollok
(made of) plastic	műanyag ...	mēwon^yog
(made of) stainless steel	rozsdamentes acél ...	rawzhdommæntæsh otsayl

Chemist's—Drugstore

In Hungarian, the name for a chemist's shop, or drugstore, is *patika* (**po**tteeko) or *gyógyszertár* (**d^yawd^y**særtaar). Their range of wares is restricted to pharmaceutical and related products—they do not sell the wide range of goods found in most British or American pharmacies.

Outside normal hours, pharmacies open on a rota basis—in larger centres there will always be at least one on night and weekend duty. An illuminated sign in each pharmacy window tells you where you can get service after hours.

For cosmetics and toiletries, go to an *illatszerbolt* (**eel**lotsærbawlt), and for photo supplies, to a *fotószaküzlet* (**faw**tāwsokewzlæt).

This section is divided into two parts:

1 Medicine, first aid, etc.
2 Toilet articles, cosmetics, etc.

General

Where's the nearest (all-night) chemist's?	Hol a legközelebbi (éjjel-nappali) patika?	hawl o **læg**kurzælæb-bee (ay^y-yæl-**nop**-pawlee) **po**tteeko
What time does the chemist's open/ close?	Mikor nyit/zár a patika?	**mee**kawr n^yeet/zaar o **po**tteeko

1 Medicines—First aid

I want something for…	Kérek valami gyógyszert … ellen.	**kay**ræk **vo**llommee d^yāwd^ysært … æl-læn
a cold	megfázás	**mæg**faazaash
a cough	köhögés	**kur**hurgaysh
a hangover	másnaposság	**maash**noppawsh-shaag
hay fever	szénanátha	**say**nonnaat-ho
insect bites	rovarcsípés	**raw**vorchēēpaysh
sunburn	napszúrás	**nop**sōōraash
travel sickness	utazási rosszullét	**oo**tozzaashee **raws**-sool-layt
an upset stomach	gyomorrontás	d^y**aw**mawr-rawntaash

DOCTOR: see page 162

Can I get it without a prescription?	Ezt recept nélkül is megkaphatom?	æst rætsæpt naylkewl eesh mægkop-hottawm
Shall I wait?	Várjak?	vaaryok
I'd like a/an/ some ...	Kérnék ...	kayrnayk
adhesive plaster	sebtapaszt	shæbtoppost
antiseptic ointment	fertőtlenítő kenőcsöt	færtūrtlænēētūr kænūrchurt
aspirins	aszpirint	ospeereent
bandage	kötszert	kurtsært
calcium tablets	mésztablettát	maystoblæt-taat
clinical thermometer	egy hőmérőt	æd^y hūrmayrūrt
contraceptives	fogamzásgátlót	fawgomzaashgaatlāwt
corn pads	tyúkszemírtót	t^{y}ōoksæmēērtāwt
cotton wool	vattát	vot-taat
cough drops	köhögés elleni cseppeket	kurhurgaysh æl-lænee chæp-pækæt
disinfectant	fertőtlenítőt	færtūrtlænēētūrt
ear drops	fülcseppeket	fewlchæp-pækæt
ear plugs	füldugót	fewldoogāwt
eye drops	szemcseppeket	sæmchæp-pækæt
first-aid kit	egy elsősegély-csomagot	æd^y ælshūrshægay^y-chawmoggawt
gauze	gézt	gayzt
insect repellent	rovarírtót	rawvorrēērtāwt
iodine	jódot	yāwdawt
laxative	hashajtót	hoshhoytāwt
nose drops	orrcseppeket	awrchæp-pækæt
painkiller	fájdalomcsillapítót	faa^{y}dollawmcheel-loppēētāwt
sanitary towels	egészségügyi vattát	ægayss-shayghews^{y}ee vot-taat
sleeping pills	altatót	oltottawt
stomach pills	gyomorfájás elleni tablettákat	d^{y}awmawrfaa^{y}aash æl-lænee toblæt-taakot
tampons	tampont	tompawnt
throat lozenges	toroköblítő tablettát	tawrawkurblēētūr toblæt-taat
tranquillizers	nyugtatót	n^{y}oogtottāwt
vitamin pills	vitamin tablettákat	veetommeen toblæt-taakot

| MÉREG! POISON! | CSAK KÜLSŐLEG! DO NOT SWALLOW! |

2 Toilet articles—Cosmetics

I'd like a/an/ some ...	Kérnék ...	kayrnayk
acne cream	egy pattanás elleni krémet	æd^y pot-tonnaash ællænee kraymæt
after-shave lotion	egy borotva kölnit	æd^y bawrawtvo kurlneet
astringent	egy borotvatapasztimsót	æd^y bawrawtvotopposteemshāwt
bath essence	egy fürdősampont	æd^y fewrdūrshompawnt
bath salts	fürdősót	fewrdūrshāwt
cologne	egy kölnit	æd^y kurlneet
cream	egy krémet	æd^y kraymæt
for dry/normal/ greasy skin	száraz/normál/ zsíros bőrre	saaroz/nawrmaal/ zhēērawsh būrr-ræ
cleansing cream	egy tisztító krémet	æd^y teestēētāw kraymæt
cuticle cream	egy bőrkrémet	æd^y būrrkraymæt
foot cream	egy lábkrémet	æd^y laabkraymæt
foundation cream	egy alapozó krémet	æd^y olloppawzāw kraymæt
hand cream	egy kézkrémet	æd^y kayzkraymæt
moisturizing cream	egy nedvesítő krémet	æd^y nædvæshēētūr kraymæt
night cream	egy éjjeli krémet	æd^y ay^y-yælee kraymæt
cuticle remover	egy bőreltávolítót	æd^y būrældtaavawlēētāwt
deodorant	egy dezodort	æd^y dæzawdawrt
emery board	egy anyósnyelvet	æd^y on^yāwshn^yælvæt
eyeliner	egy szemkihúzót	æd^y sæmkeehōōzāwt
eye pencil	egy szemöldökceruzát	æd^y sæmurldurktsæroozaat
eye shadow	egy szemkifestőt	æd^y sæmkeefæshtūrt
face pack	egy arcpakolást	æd^y ortspokkawlaasht
face powder	egy arcpúdert	æd^y ortspōōdært
foot powder	egy lábpúdert	æd^y laabpōōdært
lipsalve	egy ajakkrémet	æd^y oyok-kraymæt
lipstick	egy rúzst	æd^y rōōzht
make-up kit	egy make-up dobozt	æd^y "make-up" dawbawzt
make-up	make-up eltávolítót	"make-up" ældtaavawlēētāwt
make-up remover pads	make-up eltávolító tamponokat	"make-up" ældtaavawlēētāw tompawnawkot
mascara	egy maszkarát	æd^y moskorraat
nail brush	egy körömkefét	æd^y kurrurmkæfayt
nail clippers	egy körömvágót	æd^y kurrurmvaagāwt
nail file	egy körömreszelőt	æd^y kurrurmræsælūrt

nail polish	körömlakkot	kurrurmlok-kawt
nail-polish remover	körömlakk lemosót	kurrurmlok læmawshāwt
nail scissors	egy körömollót	æd^y kurrurmawl-lāwt
paper handkerchiefs	papírzsebkendőt	poppēērzhæbkændūrt
perfume	kölnit	kurlneet
powder	púdert	pōōdært
razor	egy borotvát	æd^y bawrawtvaat
razorblades	borotvapengéket	bawrawtvoppængaykæt
rouge	egy rúzst	æd^y rōōzht
shaving brush	egy borotvaecsetet	æd^y bawrawtvoæchætæt
shaving cream	egy borotvakrémet	æd^y bawrawtvokraymæt
shaving soap	egy borotvaszap-pant	æd^y bawrawtvossop-pont
soap	egy szappant	æd^y sop-pont
sun-tan cream	egy napozókrémet	æd^y noppāwzāwkraymæt
sun-tan oil	egy napolajat	æd^y noppawloyot
talcum powder	egy hintőport	ædy heentūrpawrt
toilet paper	w.c. papírt	waytsay poppēērt
toothbrush	egy fogkefét	æd^y fawgkæfayt
toothpaste	egy fogkrémet	æd^y fawgkraymæt
tweezers	egy csipeszt	æd^y cheepæst

For your hair

bobby pins	hullámcsattokat	hool-laamchot-tawkot
comb	egy fésűt	æd^y fayshēwt
curlers	hajcsavarokat	hoychovvorrawkot
dye	hajfestéket	hoyfæshtaykæt
hair brush	egy hajkefét	æd^y hoykæfayt
hair pins	hajtűket	hoytēwkæt
lacquer	egy hajlakkot	æd^y hoylok-kawt
oil	egy brilantint	æd^y breelonteent
setting lotion	hajlakkot	hoylok-kawt
shampoo	egy sampont	æd^y shompawnt
for dry/greasy hair	száraz/zsíros hajra	saaroz/zhēērawsh hoyro
for dandruff	korpásodás ellen	kawrpaashāwdaash æl-læn

For the baby

baby food	bébi eledelt	baybee ælædælt
bib	egy előkét	æd^y ælūrkayt
dummy (comforter)	egy cumit	æd^y tsoomeet
feeding bottle	egy cumis üveget	æd^y tsoomeesh ewvægæt
nappies (diapers)	pelenkákat	pælænkaakot
rubber teat	egy cumit üvegre	æd^y tsoomeet ewvægræ

Clothing

If you want to buy something specific, prepare yourself in advance. Look at the list of clothing on page 116. Get some idea of the colour, material and size you want. They're listed on the next few pages.

General

I'd like ... for a 10-year-old boy.	Egy ...-t kérek 10 éves fiú részére.	æd^y ...-t kayræk 10 ayvæsh feeōō rayssayræ
It's for a 6-year-old girl.	Egy 6 éves leány részére lesz.	æd^y 6 ayvæsh læaan^y rayssayræ læs
I want something like this.	Valami ilyet kérek.	vollommee ee^yæt kayræk
I like the one in the window.	Az tetszik, ami a kirakatban van.	oz tætseek ommee o keerokkotbon von
How much is that per metre?	Mibe kerül métere?	meebæ kærewl maytæræ

1 centimetre = 0.39 in.	1 in. = 2.54 cm
1 metre = 39.37 in.	1 ft. = 30.5 cm
10 metres = 32.81 ft.	1 yd.= 0.91 m

Colour

Do you have something in ...?	Van ... színűben?	von ... sēēnēwbæn
I'd like something lighter/darker.	Valami sötétebbet/ világosabbat szeretnék.	vollommee shurtaytæb-bæt/ veelaagawshob-bot sæ-rætnayk
I want something to match this.	Valami ehhez illőt keresek.	vollommee æh-hæz eel-lūrt kæræshæk
I don't like the colour.	A színe nem tetszik.	o sēēnæ næm tætseek

beige	**drapp**	drop
black	**fekete**	fækætæ
blue	**kék**	kayk
navy blue	**tengerkék**	tængærkayk
sky blue	**égszínkék**	aygsēēnkayk
brown	**barna**	borno
dark brown	**sötétbarna**	shurtaytborno
light brown	**világosbarna**	veelaagawshborno
golden	**arany**	oron^y
green	**zöld**	zurld
bottle green	**palackzöld**	pollotskzurld
lime green	**citromzöld**	tseetrawmzurld
olive green	**olivazöld**	awleevozzurld
grey	**szürke**	sewrkæ
lilac	**lila**	leelo
orange	**narancssárga**	norronchshaargo
pink	**rózsaszín**	rāwzhossēēn
red	**vörös**	vurrursh
crimson	**karmazsinvörös**	kormozheenvurrursh
purple	**bíbor**	bēēbawr
scarlet	**skarlátvörös**	shkorlaatvurrursh
silver	**ezüst**	æzewsht
turquoise	**türkiz**	tewrkeez
violet	**ibolyakék**	eebaw^{y}okkayk
white	**fehér**	fæhayr
yellow	**sárga**	shaargo
golden yellow	**aranysárga**	orron^{y}shaargo
lemon	**citromsárga**	tseetrawmshaargo
light ...	**világos ...**	veelaagawsh
dark ...	**sötét ...**	shurtayt

SHOPPING GUIDE

 sima (sheemo)

 csíkos (chēēkawsh)

 pöttyös (purt^{y}ursh)

 kockás (kawtskaash)

 mintás (meentaash)

Material

Have you anything in ...?	**... anyaguk van?**	... on^{y}oggook von
Do you have any better quality?	**Valami jobb minőségü árújuk nincs?**	vollommee yawb meenūr-shaygew aarōō^{y}ook neench

I'd like a cotton blouse.	**Egy pamutblúzt keresek.**	æd^y pommootbloozt kæræshæk
Is that ...?	**Az ...?**	oz
handmade	**kéziszöyésű**	kayzeessurvayshew
imported	**importált**	eempawrtaalt
made here	**belföldi gyártású**	bælfurldee d^yaartaashoo
What's it made of?	**Miből van?**	meeburl von

cambric	**batiszt**	botteest
camelhair	**teveszőr**	tævæssurr
chiffon	**sifon**	sheefawn
corduroy	**kordbársony**	kawrdbaarshawn^y
cotton	**pamut**	pommoot
felt	**filc**	feelts
flannel	**flanel**	flonnæl
gabardine	**gabardin**	gobbordeen
lace	**csipke**	cheepkæ
leather	**bőr**	burr
linen	**vászon**	vaassawn
rayon	**műselyem**	mewshæ^yæm
rubber	**gumi**	goomee
quilting	**tűzdelt**	tewzdælt
satin	**szatén**	sottayn
silk	**selyem**	shæ^yæm
suede	**antilop**	onteelawp
taffeta	**taft**	toft
terrycloth	**frotír**	frawteer
tulle	**tüll**	tewl
velvet	**bársony**	baarshawn^y
velveteen	**gyapjúbársony**	d^yopyoobaarshawn^y
wool	**gyapjú**	d^yopyoo
worsted	**kamgarn-szövet**	komgorn-survæt

Is it ...?	**Ez ...?**	æz
colourfast	**színtartó**	seentortaw
crease-proof	**gyűrődésmentes**	d^yewrurdayshmæntæsh
easy-care	**tiszta könnyen kezelhető**	teesto kurn^yæn kæzælhætur
pure cotton	**tiszta pamut**	teesto pommoot
shrink-resistant	**méret tartó**	mayræt tortaw
synthetic	**műanyag**	mewon^yog
wash-and-wear	**nem kell vasalni**	næm kæl vosholnee

Sizes

In Europe, sizes vary somewhat from country to country, and even within one country, so these charts must be taken as an approximate guide only.

Ladies

Dresses/Suits						
American	8	10	12	14	16	18	20
British	30	32	34	36	38	40	42
Continental	36	38	40	42	44	46	48

	Stockings						Shoes			
American } British	8	8½	9	9½	10	10½	6 4½	7 5½	8 6½	9 7½
Continental	0	1	2	3	4	5	37	38	40	41

Gentlemen

Suits/Overcoats							Shirts			
American } British	36	38	40	42	44	46	15	16	17	18
Continental	46	48	50	52	54	56	38	41	43	45

Shoes									
American } British	5	6	7	8	8½	9	9½	10	11
Continental	38	39	41	42	43	43	44	44	45

A good fit?

I take size 38.	**38-ast kérek.**	38-osht **kayræk**
May I try it on?	**Felpróbálhatom?**	fælpr$\overline{aw}$baalhottawm
It fits very well.	**Nagyon jól áll.**	nod^{y}awn y$\overline{aw}$l aal
It's too ...	**Túl ...**	t$\overline{oo}$l
short/long	**rövid/hosszú**	rurveed/**haws**-s$\overline{oo}$
tight/loose	**feszes/bő**	fæsæsh/b$\overline{ur}$
How long will it take to alter?	**Meddig tart az átalakítása?**	mæd-deeg tort oz **aat**-ollokk$\overline{ee}$taasho

Clothes and accessories

I'd like a/an/some ...	Szeretnék ...	sæarætnayk
anorak	egy anorákot	æd^y onnawraakawt
bath robe	egy fürdőköpenyt	æd^y fewrdürkurpæn^yt
blazer	egy blézert	æd^y blayzært
blouse	egy blúzt	æd^y blōōzt
bra	egy melltartót	æd^y mæltortāwt
braces	egy nadrágtartót	æd^y nodraagtortāwt
briefs	egy rövid alsónadrágot	æd^y rurveed olshaw-nodraagawt
cap	egy sapkát	æd^y shopkaat
cardigan	egy kardigánt	æd^y kordeegaant
coat	egy kabátot	æd^y kobbaatawt
dress	egy ruhát	æd^y roohaat
dressing gown	egy pongyolát	æd^y pawnd^yawlaat
evening gown	egy estélyi ruhát	æd^y æshtay^yee roohaat
frock	egy öltönyt	æd^y urlturn^yt
fur coat	egy szőrmekabátot	æd^y sūrrmækobbaatawt
gloves	egy pár kesztyűt	æd^y paar kæst^yēwt
handkerchief	egy zsebkendőt	æd^y zhæbkændūrt
hat	egy kalapot	æd^y kolloppawt
house coat	egy házikabátot	æd^y haazeekobbaatawt
jacket	egy zakót	æd^y zokkāwt
jeans	egy farmernadrágot	æd^y formærnodraagawt
jersey	egy kötöttkabátot	æd^y kurturtkobbaatawt
jumper	egy pulóvert	æd^y poolāwvært
leather trousers	egy bőrnadrágot	æd^y būrrnodraagawt
lingerie	valami alsónemüt	vollommee olshawnæmewt
mackintosh	egy esőkabátot	æd^y æshūrkobbaatawt
nightdress	egy hálóinget	æd^y haalāweengæt
overcoat	egy felöltőt	æd^y fælurltūrt
panties	egy harisnyana-drágot	æd^y horreeshn^yo-nodraagawt
pants	egy nadrágot	æd^y nodraagawt
pants suit	egy nadrágkosz-tümöt	æd^y nodraagkawstewmurt
pantyhose	egy harisnya-nadrágot	æd^y horreeshn^yo-nodraagawt
pullover	egy pulóvert	æd^y poolāwvært
pyjamas	egy pizsamát	æd^y peezhommaat
raincoat	egy esőkabátot	æd^y æshūrkobbaatawt
scarf	egy sálat	æd^y shaalot
shirt	egy inget	æd^y eengæt
shorts	egy sortot	æd^y shawrtawt
skirt	egy szoknyát	æd^y sawkn^yaat

slip	egy alsószoknyát	æd^y olshawsawkn^yaat
socks	egy pár zoknit	æd^y paar zawkneet
sports jacket	egy sportkabátot	æd^y shpawrtkobbaatawt
stockings	egy pár harisnyát	æd^y paar horreeshn^yaat
suit (man's)	egy férfiöltönyt	æd^y fayrfeeurlturn^yt
suit (woman's)	egy női ruhát	æd^y nur-ee roohaat
suspenders (Am.)	egy nadrágtartót	æd^y nodraagtortawt
sweater	egy pulóvert	æd^y poolawvært
swimsuit	egy fürdőruhát	æd^y fewrdurroohaat
tie	egy nyakkendőt	æd^y n^yok-kændurt
tights	egy harisnya-nadrágot	æd^y horreeshn^yo-nodraagawt
topcoat	egy nagykabátot	æd^y nod^ykobbaatawt
track suit	egy tréningruhát	æd^y trayneengroohaat
trousers	egy nadrágot	æd^y nodraagawt
T-shirt	egy atléta trikót	æd^y otlayto treekawt
undershirt	egy trikót	æd^y treekawt
vest (Am.)	egy mellényt	æd^y mæl-layn^yt
vest (Br.)	egy trikót	æd^y treekawt
waistcoat	egy mellényt	æd^y mæl-layn^yt

belt	öv	urv
buckle	csatt	chot
button	gomb	gawmb
collar	gallér	gol-layr
elastic	gumi	goomee
pocket	zseb	zhæb
press-stud	patentgomb	pottæntgawmb
safety pin	biztosítótű	beeztawsheetawtew
zip (zipper)	cipzár	tseepzaar

And for those handy with the needle:

crochet hook	horgolótű	hawrgawlawtew
crochet thread	horgoló cérna	hawrgawlaw tsayrno
knitting needles	kötőtűk	kurturtewk
sewing cotton	varrófonál	vor-rawfawnaal
sewing needles	varrótűk	vor-rawtewk
sewing thread	varrócérna	vor-rawtsayrno
thimble	gyűszű	d^yewssew
wool	gyapjú	d^yopyoo

Shoes

I'd like a pair of ...	Szeretnék egy pár ...	særætnayk æd^y paar
boots	csizmát	cheezmaat
galoshes	sárcipőt	shaartseepürt
hiking boots	turista bakkancsot	tooreeshto bok-konchawt
sandals	szandált	sondaalt
shoes	cipőt	tseepürt
slippers	papucsot	poppoochawt
sneakers	tornacipőt	tawrnotseepürt
tennis shoes	teniszcipőt	tæneestseepürt
These are too ...	Ez túl ...	æz tōōl
large/small	nagy/kicsi	nod^y/keechee
narrow/wide	keskeny/széles	kæshkæn^y/saylæsh
Do you have the same in ...?	Volna ugyanez ...?	vawlno ood^{y}onnæz
beige/brown	drappban/barnában	drop-bon/bornaabon
black/white	feketében/fehérben	fækætaybæn/fæhayrbæn
rubber/leather	gumiból/bőrből	goomeebāwl/bürrbürl
cloth/suede	szövetből/ antilopból	survætbürl/onteelawpbāwl
Is it genuine leather?	Ez tiszta bőrből van?	æz teesto bürrbürl von
I'd like ...	Szeretnék ...	særætnayk
pair of insoles	egy pár talpbetétet	æd^y paar tolpbætaytæt
shoe horn	egy cipőkanalat	æd^y tseepürkonnollot
shoe laces	egy pár cipőfűzőt	æd^y paar tseepürfēwzürt
shoe polish	egy doboz cipőkrémet	æd^y dawbawz tseepür- kraymæt
shoe trees	néhány kaptafát	nayhaan^y koptoffaat

Shoe repairs

Can you repair these shoes?	Meg tudná javítani ezt a cipőt?	mæg toodnaa yovvēētonnee æst o tseepürt
I want them soled and heeled.	Talpaltatni és sarkaltatni szeretném.	tolpoltotnee aysh shor- koltotnee særætnaym
When will they be ready?	Mikorra lesz kész?	meekawr-ro læss kayss

Electrical appliances and accessories

In Hungary, 220 volts, 50 cps, AC current is universal. Plugs are different from American and British ones, so you'll need to have the plugs changed on any appliances you bring from home.

I'd like a plug for this.	**Ehhez kérek egy dugaszt.**	æh-hæz **kay**ræk æd^y **doo**gost
Do you have a battery for this?	**Van ehhez elemjük?**	von æh-hæz **æl**æmyewk
This is broken. Can you repair it?	**Eltört. Meg-tudják javítani?**	**æl**turt. **mæg**tood^yaak **yov**vēētonnee
When will it be ready?	**Mikor lesz kész?**	**mee**kawr læss kayss
I'd like a/an/some ...	**Szeretnék ...**	**sær**ætnayk

adaptor	**egy adaptert**	æd^y **od**doptært
amplifier	**egy erősítőt**	æd^y **ær**ūrshēētūrt
blender	**egy keverőt**	æd^y **kæ**værūrt
bulb	**villanykörtét**	**veel**-lon^ykurrtayt
clock	**egy órát**	æd^y **āw**raat
alarm clock	**egy ébresztőórát**	æd^y **ay**bræstūrāwraat
wall clock	**egy faliórát**	æd^y **fol**leeāwraat
extension cord	**egy hosszabbítót**	æd^y **haws**-sob-bēētāwt
hair dryer	**egy hajszárítót**	æd^y **hoy**saarēētāwt
iron	**egy vasalót**	æd^y **vosh**ollāwt
kettle	**egy fazekat**	æd^y **fozz**æcot
percolator	**egy pörkölőt**	æd^y **purr**kurlūrt
plug	**egy dugaszt**	æd^y **doo**gost
radio	**egy rádiót**	æd^y **raa**deeāwt
car radio	**egy autórádiót**	æd^y **ooot**āwraadeeāwt
portable radio	**egy hordozható rádiót**	æd^y **hawr**dawz-hottāw **raa**deeāwt
record player	**egy lemezjátszót**	æd^y **læm**æzyaatsāwt
shaver	**egy borotvát**	æd^y **bawr**awtvaat
speakers	**hangfalakat**	**hong**follokkot
tape recorder	**egy magnetofont**	æd^y **mog**nætawfawnt
cassette tape recorder	**egy kazettás magnót**	æd^y **kozz**æt-taash **mog**nāwt
television set	**egy tévékészüléket**	æd^y **tay**vaykayssewlaykæt
portable TV set	**egy hordozható tévét**	æd^y **hawr**dawz-hottāw **tay**vayt
toaster	**egy kenyérpirítót**	æd^y **kæn**^yayrpeerēētāwt
transformer	**egy transzformátort**	æd^y **trons**fawrmaatawrt

Record shop

Do you have any records by ...?	**Van ...-tól/-től valamilyen lemezük?***	von ...-tāwl/-tūrl vollo-mee^{y}æn læmæzewk
May I listen to this record/cassette?	**Meghallgathatnám ezt a lemezt/kazettát?**	mægholgot-hotnaam æst o læmæzt/kozzæt-taat
I want a cassette.	**Egy kazettát kérek.**	æd^{y} kozzæt-taat kayræk
I'd like a new stylus.	**Egy új gramofontűt kérek.**	æd^{y} ōō^{y} grommawfawntēwt kayræk

LP (33 rpm)	**nagylemez**	nod^{y}læmæz
EP (45 rpm)	**kislemez**	keeshlæmæz
mono	**mono**	mawnaw
stereo	**sztereo**	stæræaw

chamber music	**kamara zene**	kommorro zænæ
classical music	**klasszikus zene**	klos-seekoosh zænæ
folk music	**népzene**	naypzænæ
instrumental music	**zenekari muzsika**	zænækorree moozheeko
jazz	**dzsessz**	dzhæs
light music	**könnyűzene**	kurn^{y}ēwzænæ
orchestral music	**zenekari darab**	zænækorree dorrob
pop music	**popzene**	pawpzænæ
rock music	**rockzene**	rawkzænæ
sacred music	**egyházi zene**	æd^{y}haazee zænæ

Here are the names of a few popular recording artists (surnames first, Hungarian style):

Bende Zsolt
Házy Erzsébet
Koncz Zsuzsa

Kovács Kati
Sass Sylvia
Zalatnai Sarolta

---

* See Grammar section for word endings.

Hairdresser's—Beauty salon

Hairdressers' work usually from 7 a.m. to 9 a.m., Monday–
Friday, and from 7 a.m. to 7 p.m., Saturday.

Is there a ladies' hairdresser/beauty salon in the hotel?	**Van a szállódában fodrászat/ kozmetikai szalon?**	von o saal-lāwdaabon fawdraassot/kawzmæteeko-ee sollawn
Can I make an appointment for (Friday)?	**Mikor jöhetek (pénteken)?**	meekawr yurhætæk (payntækæn)
I'd like a shampoo and set.	**Hajmosást kérek berakással.**	hoymawshaasht kayræk bærokkaash-shol

in a bun	**befonva**	bæfawnvo
with curls	**fürtösítve**	fewrturshēētvæ
a cut	**hajvágás**	hoyvaagash
with a fringe	**lófarokkal**	lāwforrawk-kol
page-boy style	**fiúsra vágva**	feeōōshro vaagvo
a permanent wave	**tartós hullám**	tortāwsh hool-laam

I want a …	**Kérek egy …**	kayræk æd^y
bleach	**szőkítést**	sūrkēētaysht
blow-dry	**hajszárítást**	hoyssaarēētasht
colour rinse	**bemosást**	bæmawshaasht
cut and set	**hajvágást és berakást**	hoyvaagaasht aysh bærokkaasht
dye	**festést**	fæshtaysht
shampoo	**hajmosást**	hoymawshaasht
for dry hair	**száraz hajra**	saaroz hoyro
for greasy hair	**zsíros hajra**	zhēērawsh hoyro
tint	**színezést**	sēēnæzaysht
the same colour	**ugyanilyen színűre**	ood^{y}onnee^{y}æn sēēnēwræ
a darker colour	**sötétebb színre**	shurtaytæb sēēnræ
a lighter colour	**világosabb színre**	veelaagawshob sēēnræ
Do you have a colour chart?	**Van színtáblájuk?**	von sēēntaablaa^{y}ook
I don't want any hair-spray.	**Hajlakkot nem kérek.**	hoylok-kawt næm kayræk
I want a …	**Kérek egy …**	kayræk æd^y
face pack	**arcpakolást**	ortspokkawlaasht
manicure	**manikűrt**	monneekēwrt
pedicure	**pedikűrt**	pædeekēwrt

DAYS OF THE WEEK: see page 181

SHOPPING GUIDE

Under the hair dryer, you might want to say:

It's too hot.	**Ez túl forró.**	æz tōōl fawr-rāw
A bit warmer, please.	**Egy kissé forróbbra kérem.**	æd^y keesh-shay fawr-rāwbro kayræm
Do you have any magazines?	**Van valami olvasnivalójuk?**	von vollommee awlvoshneevollāw^yook

At the barber's

I'm in a hurry.	**Sietek.**	sheeætæk
I'd like a shave.	**Egy borotválást kérek.**	æd^y bawrawtvaalaasht kayræk
I want a haircut, please.	**Egy hajvágást kérek.**	æd^y hoyvaagaasht kayræk
Cut it short, please.	**Rövidre kérem.**	rurveedræ kayræm
Don't cut it too short.	**Ne vágja túl rövidre.**	næ vaagyo tōōl rurveedræ
A razor cut, please.	**Egy borotvahajvágást, kérem.**	æd^y bawrawto-hoyvaagaasht kayræk
Don't use the electric clippers.	**Ne használja a villanyborotvát.**	næ hosnaalyo o veellon^ybawrawtvaat
That's enough off.	**Már eleget levett.**	maar ælægæt lævæt
A little more off the ...	**Még egy kicsit le lehet venni ...**	mayg æd^y keecheet læ læhæt væn-nee
back	**hátul**	haatool
neck	**a nyaknál**	o n^yoknaal
sides	**kétoldalt**	kaytawldolt
top	**felül**	fælewl
I'd like some hair lotion.	**Hajszeszt kérek.**	hoysæst kayræk
Please don't use any oil.	**Kérem, ne használjon olajat.**	kayræm næ hosnaalyawn awloyot
Would you please trim my ...?	**Kérem, vágja le a ...**	kayræm vaagyo læ o
beard	**szakállamat**	sokkaal-lommot
moustache	**bajuszomat**	boyoossawmot
sideboards (sideburns)	**pajeszomat**	poyæssawmot

TIPPING: see inside back-cover

Jeweller's—Watchmaker's

Major department stores, some small shops and private craftsmen sell costume jewellery, watches and items of folk art. The sale of gold and silver objects as well as precious stones is limited to branches of the *Óra és Ékszerbolt* chain and Intertourist shops. You may have to pay in hard currency.

Can you repair this watch?	**Meg tudják ezt az órát javítani?**	mæg **tood**^yaak æst oz a̅w̅raat yovvee̅tonnee
It's too slow.	**Sokat késik.**	**shaw**kot kay**sheek**
It's too fast.	**Nagyon siet.**	nod^yawn **shee**æt
The ... is broken.	**Eltört ...**	**æl**turrt
glass	**az üvegje**	oz **ew**vægyæ
spring	**a rugója**	o roogā̅w̅^yo
strap	**a szíja**	o se̅e̅^yo
winder	**a felhúzója**	o fælhō̅ō̅zā̅w̅^yo
The battery is flat.	**Kimerült az elem.**	**kee**mærewlt oz **æ**læm
I want this watch cleaned.	**Szeretném az órát kitisztíttatni.**	**sæ**rætnaym oz a̅w̅raat **kee**teeste̅e̅t-totnee
When will it be ready?	**Mikorra lesz kész?**	**mee**kawr-ro læss kayss
Could I see that?	**Megnézhetném?**	**mæg**nayz-hætnaym
I'm just looking round.	**Csak nézelödök.**	chok **nay**zælurdurk
I'd like a small present for ...	**Valami szerény ajándékot szeretnék ... részére.**	vollommee **sæ**rayn^y **oyaan**daykawt **sæ**rætnayk ... **ray**ssayræ
I don't want anything too expensive.	**Nem túl drágára gondolok.**	næm tō̅ō̅l **draa**gaaro **gawn**dawlawk
I'd like something ...	**Valami ... szeretnék.**	vollommee ... **sæ**rætnayk
better	**jobbat**	**yawb**-bot
cheaper	**olcsóbbat**	**awl**chā̅w̅b-bot
simpler	**egyszerűbbet**	æd^ysære̅w̅b-bæt
Is this sterling silver?	**Ez valódi ezüst?**	æz **voll**ā̅w̅dee æzewsht
How many carats is this?	**Ez hány karátos?**	æz haan^y **korr**aatawsh

Look up the name of the article you wish to buy in the following list. The lists on the next page will tell you what it's made of.

I'd like a/an/some …	Szeretnék …	særætnayk
bangle	egy karperecet	ædʸ korpærætsæt
bead necklace	egy gyöngynyakéket	ædʸ dʸurndʸnʸokkaykæt
bracelet	egy karperecet	ædʸ korpærætsæt
brooch	egy brost	ædʸ brawsht
buckle	egy csattot	ædʸ chot-tawt
chain	egy nyakláncot	ædʸ nʸoklaantsawt
cigarette case	egy cigaretta-tárcát	ædʸ tseegorræt-tottaartsaat
cigarette lighter	egy öngyújtót	ædʸ urndʸōōʸtāwt
clock	egy órát	ædʸ āwraat
alarm clock	egy ébresztőórát	ædʸ aybræstūr-āwraat
electric alarm clock	egy villany ébresztőórát	ædʸ veel-lonʸ aybræstūr-āwraat
kitchen clock	egy konyhai órát	ædʸ kawnʸho-ee āwraat
wall clock	egy faliórát	ædʸ folleeāwraat
costume jewellery	divatékszert	deevottayksært
cross	egy keresztet	ædʸ kærætsæt
cuff links	inggombot	eeng-gawmbawt
cutlery	evőeszközt	ævūr-æskurzt
ear clips	fülcsiptetőt	fewlcheeptætūrt
earings	fülbevalót	fewlbævollāwt
jewel box	egy ékszeres dobozt	ædʸ ayksæræsh dawbawzt
music box	egy zenedobozt	ædʸ zænædawbawzt
napkin ring	egy szalvéta gyűrűt	ædʸ solvayto dʸēwrēwt
necklace	egy nyakláncot	ædʸ nʸoklaantsawt
pendant	egy függőt	ædʸ fewg-gūrt
pin	egy tűt	ædʸ tēwt
powder compact	egy púdertartót	ædʸ pōōdærtortāwt
ring	egy gyűrűt	ædʸ dʸēwrēwt
engagement ring	egy eljegyzési-gyűrűt	ædʸ ælyædʸzayshee-dʸēwrēwt
signet ring	egy pecsétgyűrűt	ædʸ pæchaytdʸēwrēwt
wedding ring	egy házassági gyűrűt	ædʸ haazosh-shaaghee dʸēwrēwt
rosary	egy olvasót	ædʸ awlvoshāwt
serviette ring	egy szalvéta gyűrűt	ædʸ solvayto dʸēwrēwt
silverware	valami ezüst tárgyat	vollommee æzewsht taardʸot
snuff box	egy dohány szelencét	ædʸ dawhaanʸ sælæntsayt
tie pin	egy nyakkendő tűt	ædʸ nʸok-kændūr tēwt

watch	egy órát	æd^V a͞wraat
pocket watch	egy zsebórát	æd^V zhæbáa͞wraat
quartz watch	egy kvartz órát	æd^V kvorts a͞wraat
stopwatch	egy stopperórát	æd^V shtawp-pæráa͞wraat
wristwatch	egy karórát	æd^V korráa͞wraat
watch strap	egy óraszíjat	æd^V a͞wrossēē^{V}ot

| What kind of stone is this? | Ez milyen kő? | æz mee^{V}æn kū̄r |

amethyst	ametiszt	ommæteest
diamond	gyémánt	d^{V}aymaant
emerald	smaragd	shmorrogd
pearl	igazgyöngy	eegozd^{V}urnd^V
ruby	rubin	roobeen
sapphire	zafir	zoffeer
tiger's-eye	macskaszem (kvarc)	mochkossæm (kvorts)
topaz	topáz	tawpaaz
turquoise	türkiz	tewrkeez

| What's it made of? | Miből van? | meebūrl von |

alabaster	alabástrom	ollobaashtrawm
amber	borostyánkő	bawrawsht^{V}aankū̄r
brass	sárgaréz	shaargorrayz
copper	réz	rayz
coral	korál	kawraal
crystal	kristály	kreeshtaa^V
ebony	ébenfa	aybænfo
enamel	zománc	zawmaants
glass	üveg	ewvæg
cut glass	csiszolt üveg	cheessawlt ewvæg
gold	arany	orron^V
gold plate	aranyfüst	orron^{V}fewsht
ivory	elefántcsont	ælæfaantchawnt
jade	ékszer	ayksær
mother-of-pearl	gyöngyház	d^{V}urnd^{V}haaz
nickel silver	alpakka	olpok-ko
pewter	ón	a͞wn
platinum	platina	plotteeno
silver	ezüst	æzewsht
silver plate	ezüstlemez	æzewshtlæmæz
stainless steel	rozsdamentes acél	rawzhdomæntæsh otsayl

Laundry—Dry cleaning

If your hotel doesn't have its own laundry or dry-cleaning service, you'll have to go to a *Patyolat* (**pot**ʸawlot), an establishment which handles both laundry and dry cleaning. It may take some time, but it will certainly be quite inexpensive. Some of these shops offer express service for removing spots and stains while you wait.

Where's the nearest ...?	**Hol találom a legközelebbi ...?**	hawl tollaalawm o lægkurzælæb-bee
dry cleaner	**száraz vegytisztítót**	saaroz vædʸteestēētāwt
laundry	**mosodát**	mawshawdaat
I want these clothes ...	**Ezeket a ruhákat akarom ...**	æzækæt o roohaakot okkorrawm
cleaned	**kitisztíttatni**	keeteestēēt-totnee
washed and ironed	**kimosatni és kivasaltatni**	keemawshotnee aysh keevosholtotnee
When will it be ready?	**Mikor lesz kész?**	meekawr læss kayss
I need it ...	**... szükségem van rájuk.**	... sewkshaygæm von raaʸook
today	**Mára**	maaro
tomorrow	**Holnapra**	hawlnopro
before Friday	**Péntekre**	payntækræ
as soon as possible	**Minél hamarabb**	meenayl hommorrob
Can you mend this?	**Kijavítanák?**	keeyovvēētonnaak
Can you sew on this button?	**Felvarrná ezt a gombot?**	fælvornaa æst o gawmbawt
Can you get this stain out?	**Kivennék ezt a foltot?**	keevæn-nayk æst o fawltawt
Can this be invisibly mended?	**Meg lehet ezt láthatatlanul javítani?**	mæg læhæt æst laathototlonnool yovvēētonnee
Is my laundry ready?	**Kész van a mosnivalóm?**	kayss von o mawshneevollāwm
My name is ...	**... vagyok.**	... vodʸawk
This isn't mine.	**Ez nem az enyém.**	æz næm oz ænʸaym
There's one piece missing.	**Egy darab hiányzik.**	ædʸ dorrob heeaanʸzeek

DAYS OF THE WEEK: see page 181

Photography

I want an inexpensive camera.	**Egy olcsó fényké- pezőgépet keresek.**	æd^y awlchaw fayn^ykaypæ- zūrgaypæt kæræshæk
Do you sell home- movie cameras?	**Filmfelvevőjük van?**	feelmfælvævūr-yewrk
Show me the one in the window.	**Mutassa meg a kirakatban lévőt.**	mootosh-sho mæg o kee- rokkotbon layvūrt
I'd like to have some passport photos taken.	**Néhány útlevél- fényképet szeretnék készíttetni.**	nayhaan^y ōōtlævaylfayn^y- kaypæt særæetnayk kay- ssēētætnee

Film

It would be advisable to take some film with you to Hungary since some sizes are not available (Polaroid and 127).

I'd like a film for this camera.	**Ebbe a gépbe való filmet kérek.**	æb-bæ o gaypbæ vollaw feelmæt kayræk
black-and-white film	**fekete-fehér film**	fækætæ fæhayr feelm
colour film	**színes film**	sēēnæsh feelm
slide film	**dia-film**	deeo-feelm
cartridge	**filmpatron**	feelmpotrawn
cassette	**kazetta**	kozzæt-to
roll film	**tekercsfilm**	tækærchfeelm
120	**százhúsz**	saazhōōss
135	**százharmincöt**	saazhormeenssurt
single 8	**normál nyolc milliméteres**	nawrmaal n^yawlts meelee- maytæræsh
super 8	**szuper nyolc milliméteres**	soopær n^yawlts meelee- maytæræsh
20/36 exposures	**húsz/harmincot képes**	hōōss/hormeenssurt kay- pæsh
this size	**ez a méret**	æz o mayræt
this ASA/DIN number	**ez az ASA/DIN cikkszám**	æz oz osho/deen tseeksaam
artificial light type	**mesterséges fényérzékeny**	mæshtærshaygæsh fayn^yayrzaykæn^y
daylight type	**nappali fényre érzékeny**	nop-pollee fayn^yræ ayrzaykæn^y
fine grain	**finomszemcsés**	feenawmsæmchaysh
high speed	**nagy érzékenységű**	nod^y ayrzaykæn^yshaygēw

NUMBERS: page 175

Processing

How long will it take you to process this film?	**Mennyi ideig tart az előhívás?**	mæn^yee eedæeeg tort oz ælūrhēēvaash
How much will it cost?	**Mennyibe kerül?**	mæn^yeebæ kærewl
with a glossy/matt finish	**fényes/matt kikészítéssel**	fayn^yæsh/mot keekay-ssēētaysh-shæl
with/without border	**széllel/szél nélkül**	sayl-læl/sayl naylkewl
Will you please enlarge this?	**Kérem ezt kinagyítani.**	kayræm æst keenod^yēē-tonnee

Accessories

I want a/some ...	**Kérek ...**	kayræk
cable release	**egy kábeles kioldót**	æd^y kaabælæsh kee-awldāwt
filter	**egy szűrőt**	æd^y sēwrürt
red/yellow	**vöröset/sárgát**	vurrurshæt/shaargaat
ultraviolet	**ultraviolát**	ooltrovveeawlaat
flash bulbs	**néhány vaku-izzót**	nayhaan^y vokkoo-eez-zāwt
flash cubes	**néhány vaku-kockát**	nayhaan^y vokkoo-kawtskaat
lens	**egy lencsét**	æd^y lænchayt
lens cap	**egy lencsevédőt**	æd^y lænchævaydūrt
light meter	**egy fénymérőt**	æd^y fayn^ymayrūrt
telephoto lens	**egy teleobjektívet**	æd^y tælæawbyæktēēvæt

Repairs

This camera doesn't work. Can you repair it?	**Ez a gép elromlott. Meg tudják javítani?**	æz o gayp ælrawmlawt. mæg tood^yaak yovvēē-tonnee
The film is jammed.	**Beszorult a film.**	bæsawroolt o feelm
There's something wrong with the ...	**... nem működik.**	... næm mēwkurdeek
exposure counter	**A kioldás számláló**	o keeawldaash saamlaalāw
film winder	**A filmtekerő**	o feelmtækærūr
light meter	**A fénymérő**	o fayn^ymayrūr
rangefinder	**A távolság beállító**	o taavawlshaag bæaal-lēētāw
shutter	**A zár**	o zaar

Provisions

Here's a basic list of food and drink that you might want on a picnic or for the occasional meal in your hotel room.

I'd like some ...	Kérnék ...	kayrnayk
apple juice	almalét	olmollayt
apples	almát	olmaat
bananas	banánt	bonnaant
beer	sört	shurrt
biscuits (Br.)	kekszet	kæksæt
bread	kenyeret	kæn^yæræt
butter	vajat	voyot
cake	süteményt	shewtæmayn^yt
candy	édességet	aydæsh-shaygæt
cheese	sajtot	shoytawt
chocolate	csokoládét	chawkawlaadayt
coffee	kávét	kaavayt
cola drink	kólát	kaw̄laat
cold meat	felvágottat	fælvaagawt-tot
(a selection)		
cookies	kekszet	kæksæt
cooking fat	főzőzsírt	fūrzūrzhēert
crackers	ropogós pálcát	rawpawgāwsh paaltsaat
cream	krémet	kraymæt
cucumbers	uborkát	oobawrkaat
eggs	tojást	taw^yaasht
flour	lisztet	leestæt
frankfurters	virslit	veershleet
grapefruit	grépfrutot	graypfrootawt
grapefruit juice	grépfrut levet	graypfroot lævæt
ham	sonkát	shawnkaat
ice-cream	fagylaltot	fod^yloltawt
lemons	citromot	tseetrawmawt
lettuce	fejes salátát	tæ^yæsh shollaataat
liver sausage	májas hurkát	maa^yosh hoorkaat
milk	tejet	tæ^yæt
mineral water	ásványvizet	aashvaan^yveezæt
mustard	mustárt	mooshtaart
oil	olajat	awloyot
orange juice	narancslevet	norronchlævæt
oranges	narancsot	norronchawt
pepper	borsot	bawrshawt
pickles	ecetes uborkát	ætsætæsh oobawrkaat
potato crisps (chips)	burgonya csipszet	boorgawn^yo cheepsæt
potatoes	burgonyát	boorgawn^yaat

rolls	péksüteményt	paykshewtæmayn^yt
salad	salátát	shollaataat
salami	szalámit	sollaameet
salt	sót	shāwt
sandwiches	szendvicset	sændveechæt
sausages	kolbászt	kawlbaast
spaghetti	spagettit	shpoggæt-teet
sugar	cukrot	tsookrawt
sweets	édességet	aydæsh-shaygæt
tea	teát	tæaat
tomato juice	paradicsomlevet	porroddeechawmlævæt
tomatoes	paradicsomot	porroddeechawmawt
yoghurt	joghurtot	yawghoortawt

basket	egy kosarat	æd^y kawshorrot
bottle	egy üveget	æd^y ewvægæt
bottle opener	egy üvegnyitót	æd^y ewvægn^yeetāwt
box	egy dobozt	æd^y dawbawzt
corkscrew	egy dugóhúzót	æd^y doogāwhōōzāwt
matches	gyufát	d^yoofaat
plastic bag	egy plasztik zacskót	æd^y plosteek zochkāwt
shopping bag	egy bevásár- lótáskát	æd^y bævaashaarlāw- taashkaat
tin	egy konzervet	æd^y kawnzærvæt
tin (can) opener	egy konzervnyitót	æd^y kawnzærvn^yeetāwt
tinfoil	alufóliát	olloofāwleeaat
tube of ...	egy tubus ...-t	æd^y tooboosh ...-t

Weights and measures

1 kilogram or kilo (kg) = 1000 grams (g)

| 100 g = 3.5 oz. | ½ kg = 1.1 lb. |
| 200 g = 7.0 oz. | 1 kg = 2.2 lb. |

$$1 \text{ oz.} = 28.35 \text{ g}$$
$$1 \text{ lb.} = 453.60 \text{ g}$$

1 litre (l) = 10 decilitres (dl) or 100 centilitres (cl)
or 1000 millilitres (ml)

1 l = 0.88 imp. quarts = 1.06 U.S. quarts
1 dl = approx. ⅕ pint
2 dl = approx. ⅓ pint

| 1 imp. quart = 1.14 l | 1 U.S. quart = 0.95 l |
| 1 imp. gallon = 4.55 l | 1 U.S. gallon = 3.8 l |

Souvenirs

Hungary is a land full of fascination for souvenir- and gift-hunters. At centres throughout the country the ancient traditions of woodcarving, embroidery, weaving, pottery and other folk arts are alive and flourishing. Modern designs are found alongside age-old motifs.

Other good buys include regional costumes, local paintings, gramophone records and picture books, not to forget the many excellent local wines, fruit brandies and foodstuffs.

If you are looking for the ultimate executive toy for your boss, try the pocket-sized Hungarian "magic cube". It's a variegated cube made up of interlocking elements which you must twist around in an attempt to line up all the squares of the same colour on the same face. The endless permutations can drive even advanced mathematicians to either distraction or obsession.

carpet	**szőnyeg**	sūrn^{Y}æg
carved bowl	**faragott váza**	forroggawt vaazo
carved box	**faragott doboz**	forroggawt dawbawz
carved walking-stick	**faragott sétapálca**	forroggawt shaytoppaaltso
embroidered blouse	**hímzett blúz**	hēēmzæt blōōz
embroidered tablecloth	**hímzett asztalterítő**	hēēmzæt ostoltæreetūr
embroidery (petit point)	**hímzés**	hēēmzaysh
fruit brandy	**gyümölcspálinka**	d^{Y}ewmurlchpaaleenko
apricot brandy	**barack pálinka**	borrotsk paaleenko
cherry brandy	**cseresznye pálinka**	chæræsn^{Y}æ paaleenko
plum brandy	**szilva pálinka**	seelvo paaleenko
gramophone record	**gramofonlemez**	grommawfawnlæmæz
handicrafts	**kézmüipari termék**	kayzmeweeporree tærmayk
Herend china	**herendi porcellán**	hærændee pawrtsælaan
magic cube	**bűvös kocka**	bēvvursh kotsko
picture book	**képes kalauz**	kaypæsh kollo-ooz
pottery	**fazekastárgyak**	fozækoshtaard^{Y}ok
rug	**szőnyeg**	sūrn^{Y}æg
rustic chair	**faragott szék**	forroggawt sayk
rustic jugs	**falusi kancsók**	follooshee konchāwk
szűr (Hungarian cape)	**szűr**	sēwr
Tokay wine	**tokaji bor**	tawkoyee bawr

Tobacconist

Cigarettes, cigars and tobacco are on sale in *Dohánybolt* (**daw**haan^ybawlt) and *Trafik* (**tro**ffeek) shops, in all *ÁBC* (**aa**baytsay) and other department stores, and at most hotel counters. Intertourist branches also sell smokers' supplies, including foreign brands of cigarettes, against hard currency. Local cigarettes can be bought in packets of twenty or by the carton of 200. There are no cigarette vending machines.

Smoking is strictly prohibited in all public transport vehicles with the exception of trains, which have smokers' compartments. Cinemas, theatres and concert halls also ban smoking.

A packet of cigarettes, please.	**Kérek egy csomag cigarettát.**	kayræk æd^y chawmog tseegorræt-taat
I'd like a/an/some ...	**Kérek ...**	kayræk
cigar	**egy szivart**	æd^y seevort
cigars	**néhány szivart**	nayhaan^y seevort
cigarette case	**egy cigaretta tárcát**	æd^y tseegorræt-to taartsaat
cigarette holder	**egy szipkát**	æd^y seepkaat
cigarette lighter	**egy öngyújtót**	æd^y urndyoo^ytāwt
flints	**néhány tűzkövet**	nayhaan^y tewzkurvæt
lighter	**egy öngyújtót**	æd^y urnd^yootāwt
lighter fluid	**öngyújtó benzint**	urnd^yoo^ytāw bænzeent
lighter gas	**öngyújtó gázt**	urnd^yoo^ytāw gaast
matches	**gyufát**	d^yoofaat
packet of ...	**egy csomag ...-t**	æd^y chawmog ...-t
pipe	**egy pipát**	æd^y peepaat
pipe cleaners	**néhány pipatísztítót**	nayhaan^y peepotteesteetāwt
pipe rack	**egy pipatartót**	æd^y peepottortāwt
pipe tobacco	**pipadohányt**	peepoddawhaan^yt
pipe tool	**egy pipapiszkálót**	æd^y peepoppeeskaalāwt
tobacco pouch	**egy dohányszelencét**	æd^y dawhaan^ysælæntsayt
Do you have any ...?	**Van Önöknek ...?**	von urnurknæk
American cigarettes	**amerikai cigarettájuk**	ommæreeko-ee tseegorræt-taa^yook
British cigarettes	**angol cigarettájuk**	ongawl tseegorræt-taa^yook
menthol cigarettes	**mentolos cigarettájuk**	mæntawlawsh tseegorræt-taa^yook

I'll take 2 packets.	**2 csomaggal kérek.**	2 **chaw**mog-gol **kay**ræk
I'd like a carton, please.	**Egy kartonnal kérek.**	æd^y **kor**tawn-nol **kay**ræk
A box of matches, please.	**Egy doboz gyufát kérek.**	æd^y **daw**bawz d^y**oo**faat **kay**ræk

filter-tipped	**szűrőbetétes**	sewr**ū**rbætaytæsh
without filter	**szűrő nélküli**	sewr**ū**r naylkewlee
light tobacco	**könnyű dohány**	kurn^yew dawhaan^y
dark tobacco	**nehéz dohány**	næhayz dawhaan^y

While we're on the subject of cigarettes:

Do you mind if I smoke?	**Nem zavarja, ha dohányzom?**	næm **zov**voryo ho **daw**haan^yzawm
Would you like a cigarette.	**Parancsol egy cigarettát?**	**por**ronchawl æd^y tseegorræt-taat
Have one of mine.	**Válasszon az enyémből.**	vaaloss-sawn oz æn^y**aym**būrl
Try one of these.	**Próbálja ki ezt.**	pr**aw**baalyo kee æst
They're very mild.	**Nagyon gyengék.**	nod^yawn d^yæn**gayk**
They're a bit strong.	**Egy kissé erősek.**	æd^y **keesh**-shay ærür**shæk**

And if somebody offers you one:

Thank you.	**Köszönöm.**	**kur**surnurm
No, thanks.	**Nem kérem.**	næm **kay**ræm
I don't smoke.	**Nem dohányzom.**	næm **daw**haan^yzawm
I'm trying to give it up.	**Le akarok szokni a dohányzásról.**	læ okkorawk **sawk**nee o dawhaan^yzaashrawl
I've given it up.	**Felhagytam a dohányzással.**	**fæl**hod^ytom o dawhaan^yzaash-shol

| **DOHÁNYZÓ** SMOKING ALLOWED | **TILOS A DOHÁNYZÁS** NO SMOKING |

SHOPPING GUIDE

Your money: banks—currency

Official foreign exchange facilities can be found at: branches of the Hungarian National Bank *(Magyar Nemzeti Bank)* the National Savings Bank *(Országos Takarékpénztár—O.T.P.)* and the Hungarian Foreign Trade Bank *(Magyar Külkereskedelmi Bank),* most hotels, motels, larger campsites and tourist agencies. Some department stores and speciality shops also operate currency exchange counters.

Banking hours are generally from 9 a.m. to 5 p.m., Monday to Friday, and 9 a.m. to 2 p.m., Saturday. Keep all exchange slips. Remember to take your passport with you.

At larger exchange offices some staff usually speak English.

The unit of Hungarian currency is the *Forint* (**faw**reent), abbreviated *Ft.* It is divided into 100 *fillér* (**feel**-layr). Here are the different banknotes and coins in circulation:

Banknotes: 10, 20, 50, 100 and 500 Forints.
Coins: 10, 20 and 50 fillérs; 1, 2, 5 and 10 Forints.

Visitors may take any amount of foreign currency or traveller's cheques into or out of the country, but check before leaving with your home travel agency on possible currency registration requirements. The import and export of local currency (forints) is strictly controlled.

Exchange offices will reconvert any excess forints into the original or other foreign currencies upon your departure from the country, provided you can produce the official exchange slips you were issued at the time of the original transaction.

Most internationally recognized traveller's cheques and credit cards are accepted by official currency exchange agencies. A considerable number of tourist-oriented establishments (hotels, restaurants, shops, etc.) also take them—just look for the signs on the door.

Where?

Where's the nearest ...?	Hol a legköze- lebbi ...?	hawl o længkurzælæb-bee
bank	bank	bonk
exchange office	valuta beváltó hely	vollooto bævaaltaw hæ^y
Where can I cash a traveller's cheque (check)?	Hol lehet traveller's csekket beváltani?	hawl læhæt trovvæl-lærs chæk-kæt bævaaltonnee

At the counter

I'd like to change some ...	Szeretnék ... beváltani.	særætnayk ... bævaal- tonnee
Austrian schillings	osztrák shillinget	ostraak sheel-leengæt
Canadian dollars	kanadai dollárt	konnoddo-ee dawl-laart
German marks	nyugatnémet márkát	n^yoogotnaymæt maarkaat
pounds sterling	angol fontot	ongawl fawntawt
U.S. dollars	amerikai dollárt	ommæreeko-ee dawl-laart
What's the exchange rate?	Mi az átváltási árfolyam?	mee oz aatvaaltaashee aarfaw^yom
I'd like to cash a traveller's cheque (check).	Egy traveller's csekket szeretnék beváltani.	æd^y trovvæl-lærs chæk- kæt særætnayk bævaal- tonnee
Can you cash a personal cheque?	Személyes csekket elfogadnak?	sæmay^yæsh chæk-kæt ælfawgodnok
What rate of commission do you charge?	Mennyi az átváltási jutalék?	mæn^yee oz aatvaaltaa- shee yootollayk
How long will it take to clear?	Meddig tart a csekk ellenőrzése?	mæd-deeg tort o chæk æl-lænūrzayshæ
Can you wire my bank at home?	Táviratoznának a bankomnak?	taaveerottawznaanok o bonkawmnok
I have ...	Rendelkezem ...	rændælkæzæm
a credit card	hitelkártyával	heetælkaart^yaavol
an introduction	ajánló levéllel	oyaanlaw lævayl-læl
a letter of credit	hitellevéllel	heetæl-lævayl-læl
I'm expecting some money from home.	Hazulról várok átutalást.	hozzoolrawl vaarawk aatootollaasht
Has it arrived yet?	Megjött már?	mægyurt maar

BANK

Please give me 5000 forints in large denominations and 100 forints in small change.	**5000 forintot kérek nagy címletek- ben, továbbá 100 forintot apróban.**	5000 **faw**reentawt **kay**ræk nod^Y tsēēmlætækbæn **tawl**-vaab-baa 100 **faw**reentawt op**raw**bon
I'd like some small change.	**Aprót szeretnék.**	op**raw**t særætnayk
Could you please check that again?	**Lenne szíves újra ellenőrizni?**	**læn**-næ sēēvæsh ōō^Yro æl-lænū̄rreeznee
Could I have an exchange slip, please?	**Kaphatnék egy elismervényt?**	**kop**hotnayk æd^Y æleeshmærvayn^Yt

Depositing

I want to credit this to my account.	**Ezt az összeget szeretném a szám- lámra befizetni.**	æst oz **urs**-sægæt særætnaym o **saam**laamro bæfeezætnee
I'd like to pay this amount into Mr. ...'s account.	**Ezt az összeget ... úr számlájára sze- retném befizetni.**	æst oz **urs**-sægæt ... ōōr **saam**laa^Yaaro særætnaym bæfeezætnee
Where should I sign?	**Hol írjam alá?**	hawl ēēryom ollaa

Currency converter

In a world of floating currencies, we can offer no more than this do-it-yourself chart. You can obtain details of current exchange rates from any bank or tourist agency.

	£	$
50 fillér		
1 forint		
2 forint		
5 forint		
10 forint		
15 forint		
20 forint		
50 forint		
100 forint		

NUMBERS: see page 175

BANK

At the post office

The offices of the Hungarian postal authority *(Magyar Posta)* are open from 8 a.m. to 4 p.m., Monday–Friday, and from 8 a.m. to 1 p.m., Saturday. Main municipal and regional post offices work from 7 a.m. to 8 p.m., Monday–Saturday, sometimes with a skeleton service in the morning on Sundays and public holidays. Post offices handle mail, telephone, telegraphic and telex services, but not international money transfers.

In Budapest, a special international post, telegraph and telex office operates at the corner of Petofi Sándor utca and Martinelli-tér. It is open from 7 a.m. to 9 p.m., Monday-Friday, until 7 p.m., Saturday, and in the morning only on Sundays and public holidays.

Registered, airmail and express (special-delivery) services are available. Postal and telegraph charges, which are quite low compared with those practised in most western European countries, may be paid in forints.

Postage stamps are also on sale in tobacconists' shops. Mailboxes are red.

Few post office counter staff speak foreign languages.

Where's the nearest post office?	**Hol a legközelebbi postahivatal?**	hawl o lægkurzælæb-bee pawshtoheevottol
What time does the post office ...?	**Mikor ... a postahivatal?**	meekawr ... o pawshtoheevottol
open	**nyit**	n^{y}eet
close	**zár**	zaar
Which counter do I go to for stamps?	**Melyik ablaknál kapok bélyegeket?**	mæ^{y}eek obloknaal koppok bay^{y}ægækæt
I want some stamps.	**Bélyegeket kérek.**	bay^{y}ægækæt kayræk
I want ... 5-Ft. stamps.	**... darab 5 forintos címletet.**	... dorrob 5 fawreentawsh tsēēmlætæt

What's the postage for a letter/postcard to ...?	Mennyibe kerül egy levél/képeslap postadíja ...?	mæn^yeebæ kærewl æd^y lævayl/kaypæshlop pawshtoddēēyo
Great Britain the U.S.A.	Angliába az Egyesült Allamokba	ongleeaabo os æd^yæsewlt aal-lommawkbo
I want to send this parcel.	Szeretném feladni ezt a csomagot.	særætnaym fælodnee æst o chawmoggawt
I'd like to send this ...	... szeretném feladni.	... særætnaym fælodnee
airmail	Légipostán	laygheepawshtaan
express (special delivery)	Expressz	æxpræs
registered	Ajánlva	oyaanlvo
Where's the mailbox?	Hol a postaláda?	hawl o pawshtollaado
Do I have to fill in a customs declaration form?	Vámnyilatkozatot ki kell töltenem?	vaamn^yeelotkawzottawt kee kæl turltænæm
Where's the poste restante (general delivery)?	Hol a «poste restante» szolgálat?	hawl o pawst ræstont sawlgaalot
Is there any mail for me? My name is ...	Van posta a részemre? ... vagyok.	von pawshto o rayssæmræ. ... vod^yawk

BÉLYEGEK	STAMPS
CSOMAGFELADÁS	PARCELS
TÁVIRATOK	TELEGRAMS

Telegrams

Where's the telegram counter?	Hol lehet táviratot feladni?	hawl læhæt taaveerottawt fælodnee
I'd like to send a telegram.	Táviratot szeretnék feladni.	taaveerottawt særætnayk fælodnee
May I have a form, please?	Kaphatok egy táviró-blankettát?	kophottawk æd^y taavee-rāw-blonkæt-taat
When will the telegram be delivered?	Mikor kézbesítik a táviratot?	meekawr kayzbæshēēteek o taaveerottawt

PLACE NAMES: see page 174

Telephoning

Apart from local calls, direct dialling facilities are still the exception rather than the rule in Hungary. Among hotels, only a few five-star establishments can be reached automatically. However, modernization is proceeding apace, and each year brings an expansion of the automatic telephone network.

Local calls can be made from street pay phones. Long-distance connections are best made through your hotel switchboard operator or at a post office.

To phone abroad you'll have to ask your hotel operator to put the call through for you or go to a major post office. In Budapest you may use the convenient facilities of the international telecommunications centre at the corner of Petofi Sándor utca and Martinelli-tér.

Where's the telephone?	**Hol a telefon?**	hawl o **tælæfawn**
Where's the nearest telephone booth?	**Hol a legközelebbi telefonfülke?**	hawl o **lægkurzælæb-bee tælæfawnfewlkæ**
May I use your phone?	**Használhatom a telefonját?**	hosnaalhottawm o **tælæfawnyaat**
Do you have a telephone directory for ...?	**Van ...-i telefonkönyvük?**	von ...-ee **tælæfawnkurn^yvewk**
Can you help me get this number?	**Segítene felhívni ezt a számot?**	shæghēētænæ **fælhēēvnee** æst o **saamawt**

Operator

Do you speak English?	**Beszél angolul?**	bæsayl ongawlool
Hello, I want Boston 123-456.	**Halló! A Boston 123-456-os számot kérem kapcsolni.**	hol-lāw o **bawstawn** 123-456 awsh **saamawt** kayræm kopchawlnee
Can I dial direct?	**Lehet közvetlenül tárcsázni?**	læhæt kurzvætlænewl taarchaaznee

NUMBERS: see page 175

TELEPHONE

I want to place a personal (person-to-person) call.	Személyes beszélgetést szeretnék rendelni.	sæemay^yæsh bæsaylgæ-taysht særætnayk ræn-dælnee
A transferred-charge (collect) call, please.	«R» beszélgetést kérek.	"ær" bæsaylgætaysht kayræk
Please tell me the cost of the call when I'm finished.	A beszélgetés végén legyen szíves közölni a költséget.	o bæsaylgætaysh vaygayn læd^yæn sēēvæsh kurzurlnee o kurltshayghæt

Speaking

Hello, this is … speaking.	Halló, itt … beszél.	hol-lāw eet … bæsayl
Would you put me through to …?	Kapcsolná …-t?	kopchawlnaa …-t
I want to speak to Mr./Mrs. …	… úrral/úrnövel szeretnék beszélni.	… ōōr-rol/ōōrnurvæl særætnayk bæsaylnee
I want extension …	A …-es melléket kérem.	o …-æsh mæl-laykæt kayræm
Is that …?	Ön …?	urn
Please speak more slowly.	Legyen szíves, mondja lassabban.	læd^yæn sēēvæsh mawnd^yo losh-shob-bon

Telephone alphabet

A	Aladár	olloddaar	N	Nándor	naandawr
Á	Ágota	aagawto	O	Olga	awlgo
B	Balázs	bollaazh	Ö	Ödön	urdurn
C	Cecília	tsætsēēleeo	P	Péter	paytær
D	Dénes	daynæsh	Q	Kú	kōō
E	Erzsébet	ærzhaybæt	R	Róbert	rāwbært
É	Éva	ayvo	S	Sándor	shaandawr
F	Ferenc	færænts	T	Tivadar	teevoddor
G	Gábor	gaabawr	U	Ubul	oobool
H	Helén	hælayn	Ú	Üröm	ewrurm
I	Ilona	eelawno	V	Vilma	veelmo
J	József	yāwzhæf	W	duplavé	dooplovvay
K	Károly	kaaraw^y	X	iksz	eeks
L	László	laaslāw	Y	ipszilon	eepseelawn
M	Mónika	māwneeko	Z	Zorán	zawraan

Bad luck

Operator, you gave me a wrong number.	Központ! Rossz számot adott meg nekem.	kurzpawnt. rawss saamawt oddawt mæg nækæm
Operator, we've been cut off.	Központ! Megszakadt a beszélgetés.	kurzpawnt. mægsokkodt o bæsaylgætaysh
Would you please try again later?	Kérem, később legyen szíves újra felhívni.	kayræm kayshūrb læd\Yæn sēēvæsh ōō\Yro fælhēēvnee

Not there

When will he/she be back?	Mikor lesz benn az illető?	meekawr læs bæn oz eellætūr
Will you tell him/her I called? My name is …	Kérem, értesítse, hogy kerestem. … vagyok.	kayræm ayrtæshēētshæ hawd\Y kæræshtæm. … vod\Yawk
Would you please take a message?	Átadná az üzenetet?	aatodnaa oz ewzænætæt

---

Önt keresik telefonon.	There's a phone call for you.
Melyik számot hívja?	What number are you calling?
Kérem, tartsa a vonalat.	Please hold the line.
Foglalt a vonal.	The line is busy.
Nem veszik fel.	There's no answer.
Téves számot hív.	You've got the wrong number.
A telefon nem működik.	The phone is out of order.
Az illető jelenleg nincs bonn.	He/She is out at the moment.

TELEPHONE

Charges

What was the cost of that call?	Mibe kerül a beszélgetés?	meebæ kærewl o bæsaylgætaysh
I want to pay for the call.	Ki szeretném fizetni a telefon-beszélgetés díját.	kee særætnaym feezætnee o tælæfawnbæsaylgætaysh dēēyaat

The car

Filling station

We'll start this section by considering your possible needs at a filling station.

Petrol (gasoline), oil and diesel fuel are sold by the litre. Fuel generally come in three octane ratings—98, 92 and 86. Most filling stations will change your oil and wash your car, but they are rarely equipped for handling any repairs.

Since spare parts for Western-built vehicles are extremely difficult to obtain, it's advisable at least to take a set of some basic items with you (gaskets, fan belt, etc.) when driving to Hungary. A wise precaution is to have your car thoroughly serviced before leaving home.

Where's the nearest filling station?	**Hol a legközelebbi töltőállomás?**	hawl o laegkurzælæb-bee turltūr-aal-lawmaash
I'd like 30 litres of …	**30 liter … benzint kérek.**	30 leetær … bænzeent kayræk
98 octane	**extra**	æxtro
92 octane	**szuper**	soopær
86 octane	**normál**	nawrmaal

Fluid measures					
litres	imp. gal.	U.S. gal.	litres	imp. gal.	U.S. gal.
5	1.1	1.3	30	6.6	7.9
10	2.2	2.6	35	7.7	9.2
15	3.3	4.0	40	8.8	10.6
20	4.4	5.3	45	9.9	11.9
25	5.5	6.6	50	11.0	13.2

TIPPING: see inside back-cover

Give me 100 forints' worth of petrol (gas), please.	**Kérek 100 Forintért benzint.**	kayræk 100 fawreentayrt bænzeent
Fill the tank, please.	**Tele kérem.**	tælæ kayræm
Please check the oil and water.	**Kérem, ellenőrizze az olajszintet és a hűtővizet.**	kayræm æl-lænūrreez-zæ oz awloyseentæt aysh o hewtūrveezæt
Give me a litre of oil.	**Egy liter motor-olajat kérek.**	æd^y leetær mawtawraw-loyot kayræk
Top up the battery with distilled water, please.	**Kérem, töltse fel az akkumulátort desztillált vízzel.**	kayræm turltshæ fæl oz ok-koomoolaatawrt dæsteel-laalt vēēz-zæl
Would you check the brake fluid?	**Kérem, ellenőrizze a fékolajnyomást.**	kayræm æl-lænūrreez-zæ o faykawloyn^{y}awmaasht
Please check the tire pressure.	**Kérem, ellenőrizze a gumikat.**	kayræm æl-lænūrreez-zæ o goomeekot
1.6 front, 1.8 rear.	**1 egész 6 elöl, 1 egész 8 hátul.**	æd^y ægayss hot ælurl æd^y ægayss n^{y}awlts haatool
Please check the spare tire, too.	**Kérem a tartalék-kereket is ellenőrizni.**	kayræm o tortollayk-kæ-rækæt eesh æl-lænūrreeznee

Tire pressure			
lb./sq. in.	kg./cm²	lb./sq. in.	kg./cm²
10	0.7	26	1.8
12	0.8	27	1.9
15	1.1	28	2.0
18	1.3	30	2.1
20	1:4	33	2.3
21	1.5	36	2.5
23	1.6	38	2.7
24	1.7	40	2.8

Note: In Hungary, tire pressure is measured in kilograms per square centimetre. The following conversion chart will make sure your tires get the treatment they deserve. You can just show this panel to the filling station attendant and point to the pressures you need.

NUMBERS: page 175

CAR—FILLING STATION

Can you mend this puncture (fix this flat)?	**Kérem ezt a defektes gumit megjavítani.**	kayræm æst o dæfæktæsh goomeet mægyovēētonnee
Would you please change this tire?	**Kérem ezt az abroncsot kicserélni.**	kayræm æst oz obrawnchawt keechæraylnee
Would you please change the oil?	**Egy olajcserét kérek.**	æd^y awloychærayt kayræk
Would you clean the windscreen (windshield)?	**Lemosná a szélvédőt?**	læmawshnaa o saylvaydūrt

Miles into kilometres									
1 mile = 1.609 kilometres (km)									
miles	10	20	30	40	50	60	70	80	90	100
km	16	32	48	64	80	97	113	129	145	161

Kilometres into miles												
1 kilometre (km) = 0.62 miles												
km	10	20	30	40	50	60	70	80	90	100	110	120	130
miles	6	12	19	25	31	37	44	50	56	62	68	75	81

Have you any windscreen scrapers?	**Van szélvédő tisztítójuk?**	von saylvaydūr teestēētāw^yook
Can you sell me some antifreeze?	**Van fagyásgátló folyadékjuk?**	von fod^yaashgaatlāw faw^yoddaykyook
Could you give me small change for this?	**Adna ezért aprót?**	odno æzayrt oprāwt
Have you a road map of this area?	**Van a környékről útitérképük?**	von o kurrn^yaykrūrl ōōteetayrkaypewk
May I use your phone?	**Használhatom a telefonját?**	hosnaalhottawm o tælæfawnyaat
Where are the toilets?	**Hol a W.C.?**	hawl o vaytsay

Asking the way—Street directions

Excuse me.	**Elnézést.**	ælnayzaysht
Do you speak English?	**Beszél ön angolul?**	bæsayl urn ongawlool
Could you tell me the way to ...?	**Elmagyarázná az utat ...-ba/-be/ -ra/-re?***	ælmod^Yorraaznaa oz ootot ...-bo/-bæ/-ro/-ræ
How do I get to ...?	**Hogy jutok el ...-ba/-be/-ra/-re?***	hawd^Y yootawk æl ...-bo/-bæ/-ro/-ræ
Where does this road lead to?	**Ez az út hova vezet?**	æz oz ōōt hawvo væzæt
Can you show me on the map where I am?	**Megmutatná ezen a térképen, hogy hol vagyok?**	mægmoototnaa æzæn o tayrkaypæn hawd^Y hawl vod^Yawk
How far is it to ... from here?	**Innen milyen messze van ...?**	een-næn mee^Yæn mæs-sæ von
How far is the next town?	**Milyen messze van a legközelebbí város?**	mee^Yæn mæs-sæ von o lægkurzælæb-bee vaarawsh
Where can I find this address?	**Hogy jutok el erre címre?**	hawd^Y yootawk æl ær-ræ o tsēēmræ
Where's this?	**Ez merre van?**	æz mær-ræ von

🖝   🖘

Nem jó irányban megy.	You're on the wrong road.
Egyenesen tovább előre.	Go straight ahead.
Balra/Jobbra van, arra lenn.	It's down there on the left/right.
Menjen az első/második keresztútig.	Go to the first/second crossroads.
A közlekedési lámpánál forduljon balra/jobbra.	Turn left/right at the traffic lights.

Can you show me on the map where ... is?	**Megmutatná a tér-képen, hogy hol ...?**	mægmoototnaa o tayrkay-pæn hawd^Y hawl
Are we on the right road for ...?	**Jó úton vagyunk ... felé?**	yāw ootawn vod^Yoonk ... fælay

* See Grammar section for word endings.

In the rest of this section we'll be more closely concerned with driving conditions in Hungary and the car itself. We've divided it into two parts:

Part A contains general advice on motoring in Hungary. It would be advisable to read through it in advance.

Part B is concerned with the practical details of accidents and breakdowns. It includes a list of car parts and of things that may go wrong with them. All you have to do is to show it to the garage mechanic and get him to point to the items required.

Part A

Customs—Documentation—Other requirements

You will need the following documents in order to drive in Hungary:

● passport and visa
● valid driving licence
● car registration papers (log book)
● adequate insurance (check with your home motoring organization on latest requirements)

Motor vehicles must bear a nationality plate or sticker, clearly visible at the rear.

A red warning triangle for display on the road in case of accident or breakdown is compulsory. So is the use of safety belts in the front seats. Crash helmets must be worn by both driver and passenger of motorcycles and scooters.

Here's my ...	**Tessék ...**	tæsh-shayk
driving licence	**a jogosítványom**	o yawgawshēētvaan^yawm
insurance certificate	**a biztosítási kötvényem**	o beeztawshēētaashee kurtvayn^yæm
passport	**az útlevelem**	oz ōōtlævælæm
registration (log) book	**a gépkocsim okmányai**	o gaypkawcheem awkmaan^yo-ee

CUSTOMS, see also page 22

CAR—INFORMATION

I've nothing to declare.	**Nincs elvámolni valóm.**	neench ælvaamawlnee vollāwm
Where can I get a visa?	**Hol kapok vízumot?**	hawl koppawk vēēzoomawt

Driving—Roads

In Hungary you drive on the right and pass on the left. Go carefully until you have had time to take the measure of the local drivers—the accident rate is one of Europe's highest.

Hungary's motorways (expressways) are well maintained and toll-free. Emergency telephones for use in case of breakdown or accident are located every two kilometres (about 1¼ miles) along these roads.

Other roads are well maintained but out in the countryside not always very wide. Roads are numbered.

Traffic lights have the familiar red, yellow and green colours. You'll probably notice that the yellow stays lit longer than you're used to—but nevertheless, you are supposed to wait until it changes to green before moving off. The green light flashes several times before changing to yellow. At night, traffic lights work on a single flashing yellow, advising all drivers to pay great attention at the crossroads.

You must always stop at railway level crossings. These points are indicated by flashing red and white lights. At bridges, the vehicle closest to the approach, or already on the bridge, has priority.

Pedestrian crossings are marked with white stripes and are illuminated at night. Pedestrians have absolute priority on these crossings at all times.

Winter tires or chains are not compulsory, but driving during the November–March period without them is hazardous.

For help in case of breakdown, see page 151.

Roadsigns—Signposts

Roadsigns used in Hungary are mainly the international pictographs that are also seen on roads throughout western Europe. Some of the more important signs are shown on pages 160–161. Since they are mostly self-explanatory, they are hardly ever supplemented with written notices.

When a signboard has a smaller plate under it bearing a figure in metres, this means that the directive indicated by the roadsign only becomes effective after you have covered the distance shown.

Motorways are indicated by green signs, and other main roads by dark-blue shields. Minor roads and country lanes have signposts bearing black lettering on a white background. Signposting is generally clear.

Speed limits and some other special regulations

Speed limits for cars are: 100 kilometres per hour (62 miles per hour) on motorways, 80 kph (50 mph) on other roads outside city limits and 60 kph (37 mph) within residential areas.

Buses, heavy good vehicles, cars towing caravans (trailers) and motorcycles are restricted to 90 kph (56 mph), 70 kph (43 mph) and 50 kph (31 mph), respectively, on the three types of road specified above.

At night within residential areas, drive with your sidelights only.

If you intend to drive, don't touch a drop of alcohol: the zero limit for blood alcohol content is strictly enforced. If you are caught driving under the influence of alcohol there will be no mitigating circumstances. Penalties range from a very heavy fine to loss of your driving licence, and if you have been the cause of an accident while under the influence of drink, you are likely to end up with a stiff prison sentence.

Police

The police are normally lenient with foreign drivers, but don't push your luck. They are particularly vigilant about alcohol (see above), speeding and illegal parking in urban areas.

I'm sorry, Officer, I didn't see the sign.	**Sajnálom, uram, nem vettem észre a jelzőtáblát.**	shoynaalawm oorom næm væt-tæm aysræ o yælzūrtaablaat
The light was green.	**Zöldet mutatott a lámpa.**	zurldæt mootottawt o laampo
How much is the fine?	**Mennyi a büntetés?**	mæn^yee o bewntætaysh
Excuse me, my car has broken down.	**Elnézését kérem. Meghibásodott a gépkocsim.**	ælnayzayshayt kayræm. mægheebaashawdawt o gaypkawcheem

Parking

On the street, park your car in the direction of the traffic flow. Do not park at bus, tram (streetcar) or trolley-bus stops or at taxi ranks. Zigzag markings painted on the road surface and "no parking" signs indicate other areas where parking is prohibited. If your car has been parked in such a way as to impede traffic, it will be towed away by the police.

Budapest has parking meters, which take 1- and 5-forint coins, and guarded parking lots where you must purchase your ticket in advance.

Is there a car park in the neighbourhood?	**Van a környéken, gépkocsi parkoló?**	von o kurrn^yaykæn gaypkawchee porkawlāw
Excuse me, may I park here?	**Elnézést, szabad itt parkolnom?**	ælnayzaysht sobbod eet porkawlnawm
What's the charge for parking here?	**Mennyi itt a parkolási díj?**	mæn^yee eet o porkawlaashee dēe^y
Excuse me, have you some forint coins for the parking meter?	**Elnézest kérek, volna néhány egy-forintosa a parkoló órába?**	ælnayzaysht kayræk vawlno nayhaan^y æd^yfawreentawsho o porkawlāw āwraabo

Part B

Accidents

This section is confined to immediate aid. The legal problems of responsibility and settlement can be taken care of at a later stage. Your first concern will be for the injured.

Is anyone hurt?	**Megsérült valaki?**	mægshayrewlt vollokkee
Don't move.	**Ne mozogjon!**	næ mawzawgyawn
It's all right, don't worry.	**Nincs semmi baj, ne aggódjon.**	neench shæm-mee boy næ og-gawd^yawn
Where's the nearest telephone?	**Hol a legközelebbi telefon?**	hawl o lægkurzælæb-bee tælæfawn
May I use your telephone? There's been an accident.	**Használhatom a telefonját? Baleset történt.**	hosnaalhottawm o tælæfawnyaat. bollæshæt turrtaynt
Call a doctor/an ambulance quickly.	**Kérem, azonnal hívjon orvost/mentőket!**	kayræm ozzawn-nol hēēvyawn awrvawsht/mæntūrkæt
There are people injured.	**Többen megsérültek.**	turb-bæn mægshayrewltæk

Police—Exchange of information

Please call the police.	**Kérem, hívja a rendőrséget.**	kayræm hēēvyo o ræn-dūrrshaygæt
There's been an accident.	**Baleset történt.**	bollæshæt turrtaynt
It's about 3 kilometres from ...	**...-tól/-től körülbelül 3 kilométernyire.***	...-tāwl-tūrl kurrewlbælewl 3 keelawmaytærn^yeeræ
I'm on the Vienna–Budapest road ... of Győr.	**A Bécs–budapesti országúton vagyok Győrtől ...**	a baych boodoppæshtee awrsaagōōtawn vod^yawk d^yūrrtūrl
north/south east/west	**északra/délre keletre/nyugatra**	ayssokro/daylræ kælætræ/n^yoogotro

---

* See Grammar section for word endings.

DOCTOR: see page 162

Here's my name and address.	**Tessék a nevem és a címem.**	tæsh-shayk o nævæm aysh o tsēēmæm
Would you mind acting as a witness?	**Vállalná a tanuskodást?**	vaalolnaa o tonnooshkaw-daasht
I'd like an interpreter.	**Kérek tolmácsot.**	kayræk tawlmaachawt

B-r-e-a-k-d-o-w-n

Remember to put out a red warning triangle if the car is out of action or impeding traffic. It should be placed 50 metres behind your vehicle.

On all major roads, all year round, any driver may call for a "yellow angel"—one of the patrol cars of the Hungarian Automobile Club *(Magyar Autóklub)*. They do quick repairs at moderate prices, though they won't have any important spare parts for Western models.

This section is divided into four parts:

1 On the road
You ask where the nearest garage is.

2 At the garage
You tell the mechanic what's wrong.

3 Finding the trouble
He tells you what he thinks is the trouble.

4 Getting it repaired
You tell him to repair it and, once that's over, settle the account (or argue about it).

Phase 1—On the road

| Where's the nearest garage? | **Hol a legközelebbi javítóműhely?** | hawl o lægkurzælæb-bee yovvēētawmewhæ^Y |
| What's the telephone number of the nearest garage/"yellow angel" post? | **Mi a telefonszáma a legközelebbi javítóműhelynek/ «sárga angyal» szolgálatnak?** | mee o tælæfawnsaamo o lægkurzælæb-bee yovvēētawmewhæ^{Y}næk/ shaargo ond^{Y}ol sawlgaa-lotnok |

TELEPHONE: see page 139

CAR—REPAIRS

May I use your telephone?	Használhatom a telefonját?	hawsnaalhottawm o tælæfawnyaat
I've had a breakdown at ...	...-nál/-nél elromlott a kocsim.*	...-naal/-nayl ælrawmlawt o kawcheem
Can you send a mechanic?	Küldene egy szerelőt?	kewldænæ ædʸ særælūrt
Can you send a breakdown truck?	Tudna küldeni egy szervizkocsit?	toodno kewldænee ædʸ særveezkawcheet
How long will you be?	Meddig tart?	mæd-deeg tort
Shouldn't we call the police?	Nem szükséges a rendőrséget kihívni?	næm sewkshaygæsh o rændūrshaygæt keehēēvnee

Phase 2—At the garage

Can you help me?	Segítene?	shæghēētænæ
I don't know what's wrong with it.	Nem tudom, mije romlott el.	næm toodawm meeʸæ rawmlawt æl
I think there's something wrong with the ...	Azt hiszem, ... elromlott.	ost heessæm ... ælrawmlawt
battery	az akkumulátor	oz ok-koomoolaatawr
brakes	a fék	o fayk
bulbs	az izzók	oz eez-zāwk
cables	a vezetékek	o væzætaykæk
carburettor	a karburátor	o korbooraatawr
clutch	a kuplung	o kooploong
contact	az érintkezés	oz ayreentkæzaysh
cooling system	a hűtőberendezés	o hēwtūrbærændæzaysh
dipswitch (dimmer switch)	a reflektorkapcsoló	o ræflæktawr-kopchawlāw
dynamo	a dinamó	o deenommāw
electrical system	az elektromos berendezés	oz ælæktrawmawsh bærændæzaysh
engine	a motor	o mawtawr
exhaust pipe	a kipuffogó	o keepoof-fawgāw
fan	a ventillátor	o vænteel-laatawr
filter	a szűrő	o sēwrūr

---

* See Grammar section for word endings.

CAR—REPAIRS

fuel pump	az üzemanyag-szivatyú	oz **ewz**æmon^vogseevot^vo̅o̅
fuel tank	az üzemanyagtartály	oz **ewz**æmon^vogtortaa^v
gear shift	a sebességváltó kar	o **shæbæsh-shaygvaaltaw** kor
generator	a dinamó	o **deen**ommaw
handbrake	a kézifék	o **kay**zeefayk
headlights	a fényszórók	o **fayn**^vsawrawk
heating	a fűtés	o **few**taysh
horn	a kürt	o kewrt
ignition system	a gyujtás	o d^v**oo**^vtaash
indicator	az irányjelző	oz **eeraan**^vyælzūr
lights	a lámpák	o **laam**paak
backup lights	a hátrameneti lámpák	o **haat**rommænætee **laam**paak
brake lights	a féklámpák	o **fay**klaampaak
rear lights	a hátsóvilágítás	o **haat**shāwveelaa-ghēētaash
reversing lights	a hátrameneti lámpák	o **haat**rommænætee **laam**paak
sidelights	a városi világítás	o **vaa**rawshee veelaaghēētaash
tail lights	a hátsóvilágítás	o **haat**shāwveelaa-ghēētaash
lines (cables)	a vezetékek	o **væz**zetaykæk
lubrication system	a fékbetétek	o **fayk**bætaytæk
parking brake	a kézifék	o **kay**zeefayk
radiator	a vízhűtő	o **vēēz**hēwtūr
seat	az ülés	oz **ew**laysh
sliding roof	a tolótető	o **taw**lāwtætūr
spark plugs	a gyújtógyertya	o d^v**oo**^vtāwd^vært^vo
speedometer	a sebességmérő	o **shæbæsh-shaygmayrūr**
starter	az önindító	oz **urn**eendēētāw
steering	a kormánymű	o **kawr**maan^vmēw
suspension	a felfüggesztés	o **fælf**ewg-gæstaysh
transmission	a sebességváltó-áttétel	o **shæbæsh-shaygvaaltaw**-aat-taytæl
turn signal	az irányjelző	oz **eeraan**^vyælzūr
wheels	a kerekek	o **kær**ækæk
wipers	az ablaktörlők	oz **ob**lokturrlūrk

LEFT	RIGHT		FRONT	REAR
BALRA	**JOBBRA**		**ELÖL**	**HÁTUL**
(bolro)	(yawbro)		(ælurl)	(haatool)

It's ...

blowing	**ereszt**	æræst
broken	**eltört**	ælturrt
burnt	**kiégett**	keeaygæt
cracked	**megrepedt**	mægræpædt
defective	**hibás**	heebaash
disconnected	**szétszakadt**	saytsokkodt
dry	**száraz**	saaroz
frozen	**befagyott**	bæfod^yawt
jammed	**beszorult**	bæsawroolt
knocking	**kopog**	kawpawg
leaking	**folyik**	faw^yeek
loose	**meglazult**	mæglozzoolt
misfiring	**rossz a gyújtása**	rawss o d^yōo^ytaasho
noisy	**hangos**	hongawsh
not working	**nem működik**	næm mēwkurdeek
overheating	**túlmelegszik**	tōolmælægseek
short-circuiting	**zárlatos**	zaarlottawsh
slack	**laza**	lozzo
slipping	**csúszik**	chōosseek
stuck	**beszorult**	bæsawroolt
vibrating	**beremeg**	bæræmæg
weak	**gyenge**	d^yængæ
worn	**elkopott**	ælkawpawt

The car won't start. | **Nem indul.** | næm eendool

It's locked and the keys are inside. | **Be van zárva és a kulcsok belül vannak.** | bæ von zaarvo aysh o koolchawk bælewl von-nok

The battery is flat. | **Az akkumulátor kimerült.** | oz ok-koomoolaatawr keemærewlt

The fan belt is too slack. | **A ventillátor-szíj nagyon laza.** | o vænteel-laatawr sēe^y nod^yawn lozzo

I want my car serviced and lubricated. | **Karbantartást és zsírzást kérek.** | korbontortaasht aysh zhēērzaasht kayræk

The idling needs adjusting. | **Az alapjáratot be kell állítani.** | oz ollopyaarottawt bæ kæl aal-lēētonnee

The pedals need adjusting. | **A pedált szükséges beállítani.** | o pædaalt sewkshaygæsh bæaal-lēētonnee

The steering wheel is vibrating. | **A kormánykerék beremeg.** | o kawrmaan^ykærayk bæræmæg

The wipers are smearing. | **Az ablaktörlők maszatolnak.** | oz oblokturrlūrk mossottawlnok

Now that you've explained what's wrong:

How long will it take to repair?	**Meddig tart a javítás?**	mæd-deeg tort o yovvēē-taash
Can you give me a ride into town?	**Elvinne a városba?**	ælveen-næ o vaarawshbo
Could you get me a taxi?	**Hívna nekem egy taxit?**	hēēvno nækæm æd^y toxeet
Is there a hotel nearby?	**Van a környéken szálloda?**	von o kurn^{y}aykæn saal-lawdo

Phase 3—Finding the trouble

If you don't know what's wrong with the car, it's up to the mechanic to find the trouble. You can ask him what has to be repaired by handing him the book and pointing to the Hungarian text below.

Kérem, tekintse végig a következő, ábécé sorrendben összeállított listát és mutasson rá a meghibásodott tételre. Ha az ügyfele a hiba okát is tudni kívánja, válassza ki a megfelelő kifejezést a következő listából (eltört, zárlatos stb.).*

adagoló	injection pump
akkumulátor	battery
akkumulátor cellák	battery cells
automata sebességváltó	automatic transmission
betét	lining
csapágy	bearing
csapszeg	stems
csatlakozó	connection
desztillált víz	distilled water
dinamó	dynamo, generator
dugattyú	piston
dugattyú gyűrű	piston ring
elosztó kábel	distributor leads

---

* Please look at the following alphabetical list and point to the defective item. If your customer wants to know what's wrong with it, pick the applicable term from the next list (broken, short-circuited, etc.).

CAR—REPAIRS

érintkezési pont	contact
felfüggesztés	suspension
felfüggesztő gyűrű	suspension ring
felfüggesztő rugó	suspension spring
fék	brakes
fékdob	brake drum
fékpofa	brake shoes
féktárcsa	brake disc
fogastengely	rack and pinion
fogazás	teething
főcsapágy	main bearing
főtengely	camshaft
függesztőmű	stabilizer
gyertya	spark plug
gyertyakábel	plug leads
gyújtás	ignition
gyűrű	ring
hajtómű	transmission
henger	cylinder
hengerfej	cylinder head
hengerfej tömítés	cylinder head gasket
hűtőberendezés	cooling system
illesztés	joints
indító motor	starter motor
karburátor	carburettor
kardánház	crankcase
kardántengely	crankshaft
kardán vezérlés	universal joint
kábel	cable
kondenzátor	capacitor
kormány	steering column
kormánymű	steering system
kuplung	clutch
kuplung pedál	clutch pedal
lengéscsillapító	shock absorber
légrugózás	pneumatic suspension
légszűrő	air filter
membrán	diaphragm
motor	engine
motorház	engine block
olajszivattyú	oil pump
olajszűrő	oil filter
radiátor	radiator
reflektor kapcsoló	dipswitch (dimmer switch)
rugók	springs
sebességváltó	gearbox

szelep emelő	tappet
szeleptest	valve
szivattyú	pump
szűrő	filter
tengely	shaft
termosztát	thermostat
úszó	float
üzemanyag szivattyú	petrol (gas) pump
üzemanyag szűrő	petrol (gas) filter
ventillátor	fan
ventillátor szíj	fan belt
villamos berendezés	electrical system
vízszivattyú	water pump

A következő lista azokat a kifejezéseket tartalmazza, amelyek a hibákat és a kijavítás módját magyarázzák meg.*

alacsony	low
áteresztés	blowing
beállítani	to adjust
becsiszolni	to grind in
befagyott	frozen
beszorult	jammed, stuck
csúszás	sliding
defekt	puncture
elégett	burnt
elgörbült	deformed, bent, warped
elkopott	chipped, worn
eltört	broken
feltölteni	to charge
folyás	leaking
gyenge	weak
gyors	quick
gyújtáshiba	misfiring
hegeszteni	to weld
hibás	defective
holtjáték	play
kicserélni	to change, replace
kiegyensúlyozni	to balance
kiereszteni	to bleed
kiégett	blown
kiszerelni	to strip down
kiugrott	cracked

---

* The following list contains words which describe what's wrong as well as what may need to be done.

kopogás	knocking
laza	slack, loose
magas	high
meghúzni	to tighten
meglazítani	to loosen
megrozsdásodott	corroded
piszkos	dirty
rezgés	vibration
rövid	short
száraz	dry
szénteleníteni	to decarbonize
szétment	disconnected
túlmelegedés	overheating
újrabélelni	to reline
üres	empty
zárlatos	short-circuited
zsírozni	to grease

Phase 4—Getting it repaired

Have you found the trouble?	**Megvan a hiba?**	**mæg**von o **hee**bo
Is it serious?	**Komoly?**	**kaw**maw^y
Can you repair it?	**Meg tudják javítani?**	mæg **tood**^{y}aak **yov**vēētonnee
Can you repair it at once?	**Meg tudják rögtön javítani?**	mæg **tood**^{y}aak **rurg**turn **yov**vēētonnee
What's it going to cost?	**Mennyibe kerül?**	**mæn**^{y}eebæ **kæ**rewl
Do you have the necessary spares?	**Van alkatrészük hozzá?**	von **ol**kotrayssewk **hawz**-zaa

What if he says "no"?

Why can't you do it?	**Miért nem tudják megjavítani?**	**mee**ayrt næm **tood**^{y}aak **mæg**yovvēētonnee
Is it essential to have that part?	**Feltétlenül szükséges az az alkatrész?**	**fæl**taylænewl **sewk**shaygæsh oz oz **ol**kotrayss
How long is it going to take to get the spare parts?	**Meddig tart beszerezni az alkatrészeket?**	**mæd**-deeg tort **bæ**særæznee oz **ol**kotrayssækæt

Where's the nearest garage that can repair it?	Hol a legközelebbi szerviz, ahol meg tudják javítani?	hawl o lægkurzælæb-bee særveez ohawl mæg tood^yaak yovvēētonnee
Can you fix it so that I can get as far as ...?	Rendbe tudják annyira hozni, hogy ...-ig eljuthassak vele?	rændbæ tood^yaak on^yeero hawznee hawd^y ...-eeg ælyoot-hosh-shok vælæ

If you're really stuck, ask if you can leave the car at the garage. Don't forget to empty it of valuables. Contact the Hungarian Automobile Association or hire another car.

Settling the bill

Is everything all right?	Minden rendben?	meendæn rændbæn
How much do I owe you?	Mennyivel tartozom?	mæn^yeevæl tortawzawm
Do you accept traveller's cheques (checks)?	Traveller's csekket elfogadnak?	trovvæl-lærs chæk-kæt ælfawgodnok
Can I pay with this credit card?	Fizethetek ezzel a hitelkártyával?	feezæt-hætæk æz-zæl o heetælkaart^yaavol
Do you accept foreign money?	Külföldi valutát elfogadnak?	kewlfurldee vollootaat ælfawgodnok
I have to change some money.	Pénzt kell váltanom.	paynzt kæl vaaltonnawm
Thanks very much for your help.	Köszönöm szépen a segítségét.	kursurnurm saypæn o shæghēētshaygayt

But you may feel that the workmanship is sloppy or that you're paying for work not done. In that case, get the bill itemized. If necessary have it translated before you pay.

I'd like to check the bill first.	Először szeretném ellenőrizni a számlát.	ælūrssurr særætnaym æl-lænūrreeznee o saamlaat
Will you itemize the work done?	Részleteznék az elvégzett munkát?	rayslætæznayk oz ælvaygzæt moonkaat

Some international road signs

No vehicles

No entry

No overtaking (passing)

Oncoming traffic has priority

Maximum speed limit

No parking

Caution

Intersection

Dangerous bend (curve)

Road narrows

Intersection with secondary road

Two-way traffic

Dangerous hill

Uneven road

Falling rocks

Give way (yield)

Main road,
thoroughfare

End of
restriction

One-way traffic

Traffic goes
this way

Roundabout
(rotary)

Bicycles
only

Pedestrians
only

Minimum
speed limit

Keep right
(left if symbol
reversed)

Parking

Hospital

Motorway
(expressway)

Motor
vehicles only

Filling
station

No through
road

Doctor

Frankly, how much use is a phrase book going to be to you in case of serious illness or injury? The only phrase you need in such an emergency is:

| Get a doctor quickly! | **Kérem, azonnal hívjon orvost!** | kayræm ozzawn-nol hēēvyawn awrvawsht |

But there are minor aches and pains, ailments and irritations, that can upset the best planned trip. Here we can help you—and, perhaps, the doctor.

Some doctors may speak a little English. At any rate, they are likely to know enough medical terminology in English for your needs. But suppose there's something the doctor cannot explain because of language difficulties? We've thought of that. As you'll see, this section has been arranged to enable you and the doctor to communicate. From page 165 to page 171, you'll find your part of the dialogue on the upper half of each page—the doctor's is on the lower half.

The whole section is divided into three parts: illness, wounds, nervous tension. Page 171 is concerned with prescriptions and fees. The phrases on pages 172 and 173 will be of help to you at the dentist's or the optition's.

General

Can you get me a doctor?	**Tudna hívni orvost?**	toodno hēēvnee awrvawsht
Is there a doctor here who speaks English?	**Van angolul beszélő orvosuk?**	von ongawlool bæsaylūr awrvawshook
Where's the surgery (doctor's office)?	**Hol az orvosi rendelő?**	hawl oz awrvawshee rændælūr
What are the surgery (office) hours?	**Mikor rendel?**	meekawr rændæl
Could the doctor come to see me here?	**Kihívható az orvos hozzám?**	keehēēvhottāw oz awrvawsh hawz-zaam

PHARMACY: see page 108

The Hungarian National Health Service, widely known by its abbreviation *Sz. T. K.* (**æ**staykaa), or the special emergency squad *Mentők* (**mæn**tūrk) provide all necessary help, including hospitalization, in case of emergency. Medical standards are in general very high. Most doctors and dentists also have private practices, and many foreigners go to Hungary to enjoy private medical and dental care at relatively low cost.

Symptoms

Use this section to tell the doctor what's wrong. Basically, what he'll require to know is:

What?	(ache, pain, bruise, etc.)
Where?	(arm, stomach, etc.)
How long?	(have you had the trouble)

Before you visit the doctor find out the answers to these questions by glancing through the pages that follow. In this way you'll save time.

Parts of the body

ankle	**boka**	bawko
appendix	**vakbél**	vokbayl
arm	**kar**	kor
artery	**ütőér**	ewtūr-ayr
back	**hát**	haat
bladder	**hólyag**	hāw^yog
blood	**vér**	vayr
bone	**csont**	chawnt
bowels	**has**	hosh
breast	**mell**	mæl
cheek	**arc**	orts
chest	**mellkas**	mælkosh
chin	**áll**	aal
collar-bone	**kulcs-csont**	koolch-chawnt
ear	**fül**	fewl
elbow	**könyök**	kurn^yurk
eye	**szem**	sæm
face	**arc**	orts
finger	**ujj**	oo^y

DOCTOR

foot	lábfej	laabfæ^y
forehead	homlok	hawmlawk
genitals	nemi szervek	næmee særvæk
gland	mirigy	meereed^y
hair	haj	hoy
hand	kéz	kayz
head	fej	fæ^y
heart	szív	sēēv
heel	sarok	shorrawk
hip	csípő	chēēpūr
intestines	belek	bælæk
jaw	állkapocs	aalkoppawch
joint	ízület	ēēzewlæt
kidney	vese	væshæ
knee	térd	tayrd
knee-cap	térdkalács	tayrdkollaach
leg	láb	laab
lip	ajak	oyok
liver	máj	maa^y
lung	tüdő	tewdūr
mouth	száj	saa^y
muscle	izom	eezawm
neck	nyak	n^yok
nerve	ideg	eedæg
nervous system	idegrendszer	eedægrændsær
nose	orr	awr
rib	borda	bawrdo
shoulder	váll	vaal
skin	bőr	būrr
spine	hátgerinc	haatgæreents
stomach	gyomor	d^yawmawr
tendon	ín	ēēn
thigh	comb	tsawmb
throat	torok	tawrawk
thumb	hüvelyk	hewvvæ^yk
toe	lábujj	laaboo^y
tongue	nyelv	n^yælv
tonsils	mandula	mondoolo
urine	vizelet	veezælæt
vein	ér	ayr
wrist	csukló	chooklāw

LEFT/ON THE LEFT SIDE	RIGHT/ON THE RIGHT SIDE
BAL/A BALOLDALON	**JOBB/A JOBB OLDALON**
(hol/o **bol**lawldollawn)	(yawb/o yawb **awl**dollawn)

PATIENT
Part 1—Illness

I'm not feeling well.	**Rosszul érzem magam.**	rawss-sool ayrzæm moggom
I'm ill.	**Beteg vagyok.**	bætæg vod^{Y}awk
I've got a pain here.	**Itt fáj valami.**	eet faa^Y vollommee
I've got a fever.	**Lázas vagyok.**	laazosh vod^{Y}awk
I've got a ...	**Fáj a ...**	faa^Y o
backache	**hátam**	haatom
headache	**fejem**	fæ^{Y}æm
sore throat	**torkom**	tawrkawm
stomachache	**gyomrom**	d^{Y}awmrawm
I've been vomiting.	**Hánytam.**	haan^{Y}tom
I'm constipated.	**Verítékezem.**	væreeetaykæzæm

DOCTOR
Első rész—Betegség

Mi a panasza?	What's the trouble?
Hol fáj?	Where does it hurt?
Milyen fájdalmat érez?	What kind of pain is it?
tompa/éles/lüktető állandó/változó	dull/sharp/throbbing constant/on and off
Mióta érzi így magát?	How long have you been feeling like this?
Tűrje fel az ingujját.	Roll up your sleeve, please.
Kérem vetkőzzön le (derékig).	Please undress (down to the waist).

DOCTOR

PATIENT

I feel dizzy.	**Szédülök.**	saydewlurk
I feel faint.	**Gyengének érzem magamat.**	d^{y}ængaynæk ayrzæm moggommot
I feel shivery.	**Ráz a hideg.**	raaz o **hee**dæg
I feel nauseous.	**Hányingerem van.**	haan^{y}eengæræm von
I've got ... degrees temperature.	**... fok lázam van.**	... fawk **laa**zom von
I've got (a/an) ...		
asthma	**Asztmás vagyok.**	**ost**maash vod^{y}awk
bronchitis	**Bronhitiszem van.**	brawnheeteessæm von
cold	**Meg vagyok fázva.**	mæg vod^{y}awk **faa**zvo
cough	**Köhögök.**	kurhurgurk
cramps	**Görcsölök.**	gurrchurlurk
diarrhoea	**Megy a hasam.**	mæd^y o hoshom
earache	**A fülem fáj.**	o **few**læm faa^y
haemorrhoids	**Aranyerem van.**	orron^{y}æræm von
hayfever	**Szénanáthám van.**	saynonnaat-haam von
heartburn	**Gyomorégésem van.**	d^{y}awmawraygayshæm von

DOCTOR

Kérem, feküdjön le ide.	Please lie down over there.
Nyissa ki a száját.	Open your mouth.
Sóhajtson mélyeket.	Breathe deeply.
Köhögjön kérem.	Cough, please.
Megmérem a vérnyomását/a lázát.	I'll take your blood pressure/ temperature.
Először van ilyen állapotban?	Is this the first time you've had this?
Adok egy injekciót.	I'll give you an injection.
Vér/Széklet/Vizelet mintára van szükségem.	I want a specimen of your blood/stools/urine.
... napig ágyban kell maradnia.	You must stay in bed for ... days.

PATIENT

hernia	**Sérvem van.**	shayrvæm von
indigestion	**Gyomorrontásom van.**	d^yawmawr-rawntaashawm von
an itch	**Viszketegségem van.**	veeskætægshaygæm von
nosebleed	**Vérzik az orrom.**	vayrzeek oz awr-rawm
palpitations	**Szívdobogásom van.**	sēēvdawbawgaashawm von
period pains	**Menstruálok.**	mænshtrooaalawk
rash	**Kiütéses vagyok.**	keeewtayshæsh vod^yawk
rheumatism	**Reumás vagyok.**	ræoomaash vod^yawk
shivers	**Ráz a hideg.**	raaz o heedæg
stiff neck	**Nyakmerevedésem van.**	n^yokmærævædayshæm von
sunstroke	**Napszúrásom van.**	nopsōōraashawm von
ulcer	**Fekélyem van.**	fækay^yæm von
It's nothing serious, I hope.	**Remélem, semmi komoly.**	ræmaylæm shæm-mee kawmaw^y
Is it contagious?	**Fertőző?**	færtūrzūr
I'd like you to prescribe some medicine for me.	**Kérem írjon fel a részemre néhány orvosságot.**	kayræm ēēryawn fæl o rayssæmræ nayhaan^y awrvawsh-shaagawt

---

DOCTOR

Semmi komoly.	It's nothing serious.
Önnek ...	You've got ...
ételmérgezése	food poisoning
gyomorhurutja van	gastritis
... gyulladása van	inflammation of ...
hólyaggyulladása	cystitis
homloküreggyulladása van	sinusitis
influenzája van	flu
ízületi gyulladás	arthritis
középfülő gyulladása van	inflammation of the middle ear
megfázásos hasmenése	gastric flu
tüdőgyulladása van	pneumonia
vakbélgyulladása	appendicitis
veseköve van	biliary colics
Önnek szakorvoshoz kell mennie.	I want you to see a specialist.

PATIENT

I'm a diabetic.	**Cukorbeteg vagyok.**	tsookawrbætæg vod^yawk
I've a cardiac condition.	**Szívbántalmaim vannak.**	sēēvbaantolmo-eem von-nok
I had a heart attack ... years ago.	**... évvel ezelőt szívrohamom volt.**	... ayv-væl æzælūrt sēēvrawhommawm vawlt
I'm allergic to ...	**Allergiás vagyok ...-ra/-re.***	ol-lærgheeaash vod^yawk ...-ro/-ræ
This is my usual medicine.	**Ezt a gyógyszert szoktam szedni.**	æst o d^yāwd^ysært sawktom sædnee
I need this medicine.	**Erre a gyógyszerre van szükségem.**	ær-ræ o d^yāwd^ysær-ræ von sewkshaygæm
I'm expecting a baby.	**Terhes vagyok.**	tærhæsh vod^yawk
I'm in my ... month.	**A ...-dik hónapban vagyok.**	o ...-deek hāwnopbon vod^yawk
Can I travel?	**Utaznom szabad?**	ootoznawm sobbod

DOCTOR

Milyen adag inzulint kap?	What dose of insulin are you taking?
Injekcióban, vagy szájon át?	Injection or oral?
Hogy kezelik jelenleg?	What treatment are you having?
Milyen gyógyszert szed?	What medicine are you taking?
Általában mennyit szed?	What's your normal dose?
(Enyhe) szívrohama volt.	You've had a (mild) heart attack.
...-t Magyarországon nem használjuk. Ez hasonló.	We don't use ... in Hungary. This is similar.
Mikorra esedékes a szülés?	When is the baby due?
...-ig nem utazhat.	You can't travel until ...

---

* See Grammar section for word endings.

PATIENT
Part 2—Wounds

Could you have a look at this ...?	**Megvizsgálná ezt a ...?**	mægveezhgaalnaa æst o
bite	**harapást**	horroppaasht
blister	**hólyagot**	hawᵞoggawt
boil	**kelést**	kælaysht
bruise	**zúzódást**	zōōzāwdaasht
burn	**égést**	aygaysht
cut	**vágást**	vaagaasht
graze	**horzsolást**	hawrzhawlaasht
insect bite	**rovarcsípést**	rawvorcheēpaysht
lump	**csomót**	chawmāwt
rash	**kiütést**	keeewtaysht
sore	**sebet**	shæbæt
sting	**csípést**	cheēpaysht
swelling	**daganatot**	doggonnottawt
wound	**sebet**	shæbæt

| I can't move ... | **Nem tudok mozogni** | næm toodawk |
| It hurts. | **a ... Fáj.** | mawzawgnee o ... faaᵞ |

DOCTOR
2. rész—Sebesülés

(Nem) fertőzött.	It's (not) infected.
Porckorongsérve/Isiásza van.	You've got a slipped disc/sciatica.
Meg kell önt röntgeneztetnem.	I'd like you to have an X-ray.
Ez ...	It's ...
eltört/kiugrott	broken/dislocated
elszakadt/kificamodott	torn/sprained
Izomrándulása van.	You've pulled a muscle.
Antiszeptikumot/ Fájdalomcsillapítót adok Önnek.	I'll give you an antiseptic/a painkiller.
Tetanusz ellen már oltották?	Have you been vaccinated against tetanus?
Kérem, hogy ... nap múlva jöjjön vissza.	I'd like you to come back in ... days.

PARTS OF THE BODY: see page 163

DOCTOR

PATIENT

Part 3—Nervous tension

I'm in a nervous state.	**Ideges vagyok.**	eedægæsh vod^yawk
I'm feeling depressed.	**Depressziós a hangulatom.**	dæpræs-seeāwsh o hongoolottawm
I'm suffering from anxiety.	**Izgatott vagyok.**	eezgottawt vod^yawk
I can't eat.	**Nem tudok enni.**	næm toodawk æn-nee
I can't sleep.	**Nem tudok aludni.**	næm toodawk olloodnee
Can you prescribe ...?	**Felírna valami ...?**	fæleērno vollommee
an antidepressant	**depresszió elleni szert**	dæpræs-seeāw æl-lænee sært
some sleeping pills	**altatót**	oltottāwt
a tranquillizer	**nyugtatót**	n^yoogtottāwt
I don't want anything too strong.	**Kérem, ne adjon túl erős orvosságot.**	kayræm næ odyawn tōōl ærūūrsh awrvawsh-shaagawt

---

DOCTOR

3. rész—Idefeszültség

Ön idegfeszültségben. szenved.	You're suffering from nervous tension.
Pihenésre van szüksége.	You need a rest.
Milyen gyógyszert szedett eddig?	What pills have you been taking?
Naponta hányat?	How many a day?
Mióta érzi így magát?	How long have you been feeling like this?
Felírok néhány tablettát.	I'll prescribe some pills.
Adok Önnek nyugtatót/ altatót.	I'll give you a tranquillizer/ some sleeping pills.
Ezzel kihúzza amíg hazaér.	This will see you through until you get home.

DOCTOR

PATIENT

Prescription and dosage

What kind of medicine is this?	**Ez milyen orvosság?**	æz mee^{Y}æn awrvawsh-shaag
How many times a day should I take it?	**Naponta hányszor szedjem?**	noppawnto haan^{Y}sawr sæd^{Y}æm
Must I swallow them whole?	**Egészben kell lenyelnem?**	ægaysbæn kæl læn^{Y}æl-næm

Fee

How much do I owe you?	**Mennyivel tartozom?**	mæn^{Y}eevæl tortawzawm
Do I pay you know or will you send me your bill?	**Most fizessek, vagy elküldi a számláját?**	mawsht feezæsh-shæk vod^Y ælkewldee o saam-laa^{Y}aat
May I have a receipt for my health insurance?	**Kaphatok egy elismervényt a biztosítóm részére?**	kophottawk æd^Y æl-eeshmærvayn^{Y}t o beez-tawshēētāwm rayssayræ

DOCTOR

Gyóggszertelírás és adagolás

Ebből az orvosságból ... káveskanállal szedjen.	Take ... teaspoons of this medicine.
... tablettát vegyen be minden ...-ik órában egy pohár vízzel.	Take ... pills with a glass of water every ... hours.
minden étkezés előtt	before each meal
minden étkezés után	after each meal
reggelente/esténként	in the morning/at night
mikor fájdalmai vannak	in case of pain
... napig	for ... days

Tiszteletdíj

Tudna most fizetni?	Can you pay me now, please?
Elküldöm Önnek a számlát.	I'll send you the bill.

NUMBERS: page 175

Dentist

Can you recommend a good dentist?	Ajánlana egy jó fogorvost?	oyaanlonno ædᵛ yā̄w fawgawrvawsht
Can I make an (urgent) appointment to see Doctor ...?	(Sürgősen) mikor kereshetem fel doktor ...-t?	(shewrgū̄rshæn) meekawr kæræshhætæm fæl dawktawr ...-t
Can't you possibly make it earlier than that?	Nem lehetne hamarabb?	næm læhætnæ hommorrob
I've a toothache.	Fáj a fogam.	faaᵛ o fawgom
I've an abscess.	Tályogos a fogam.	taaᵛawgawsh o fawgom
This tooth hurts.	Ez a fogam fáj.	æz o fawgom faaᵛ
at the top	fent	fænt
at the bottom	lent	lænt
in the front	elöl	ælurl
at the back	hátul	haatool
Can you fix it up temporarily?	Ideiglenesen rendbe tudná hozni?	eedæeeglænæshæn rændbæ toodnaa hawznee
Please give me a local anaesthetic.	Kérem, adjon helyi érzéstelenítést.	kayræm odᵛawn hæᵛee ayrzayshtælænē̄ē̄taysht
I don't want it extracted.	Nem akarom kihúzatni.	næm okkorrawm keehō̄ō̄zotnee
I've lost a filling.	Kiesett egy tömítésem.	keeæshæt ædᵛ turmē̄ē̄taysham
The gum is ...	... az ínyem.	... oz ē̄ē̄nᵛæm
bleeding	Vérzik	vayrzeek
sore	Sebes	shæbæsh

Dentures

I've broken my denture.	Eltörtem a műfogsoromat.	ælturrtæm o mēw̄fawgshawrawmot
Can you repair this denture?	Meg tudná javítani?	mæg toodnaa yovvē̄ē̄tonnee
When will it be ready?	Mikor lesz kész?	meekawr læss kayss

Optician

Where can I find an optician?	Hol találok egy optikust?	hawl tollaalawk æd^y awpteekoosht
I've broken my glasses.	Eltörtem a szemüvegemet.	ælturrtæm o sæmewvægæmæt
Can you repair them for me?	Meg tudná javítani?	mæg toodnaa yovvēētonnee
When will they be ready?	Mikor lesz kész?	meekawr læss kayss
Can you change the lenses?	Ki tudja cserélni az üvegeket?	kee tood^yo chæraylnee oz ewvægækæt
I'd like tinted lenses.	Színes üveget szeretnék.	sēēnæsh ewvægæt særætnayk
I'd like to have my eyesight checked.	Szeretném megvizsgáltatni a szememet.	særætnaym mægveezhgaaltotnee o sæmæmæt
I'm short-sighted/long-sighted.	Rövidlátó/Távolbalátó vagyok.	rurveedlaataw/taavawlbolaataw vod^yawk
I'd like a spectacle case.	Egy szemüvegtartót kérnék.	æd^y sæmewvægtortāwt kayrnayk
I've lost a contact lens.	Elvesztettem az egyik kontakt üvegemet.	ælvæstæt-tæm oz æd^yeek kawntokt ewvægæmæt
I've hard/soft lenses.	Kemény/Puha lencséim vannak.	kæmayn^y/pooho lænchayeem von-nok
Could you give me another lens?	Tudna másik lencsét adni?	toodno maasheek lænchayt odnee
Have you got some liquid for contact lenses?	Van kontakt lencséhez szemcseppjük?	von kawntokt lænchayhæz sæmchæpyewk
A small/large bottle, please.	Egy kis/nagy üveggel kérek.	æd^y keesh/nod^y ewvæg-gæl kayræk
I'd like a pair of sunglasses.	Egy napszemüveget kérek.	æd^y nopsæmewvægæt kayræk
May I look in a mirror?	Megnézhetem magam a tükörben?	mægnayz-hætæm moggom o tewkurrbæn
I'd like a pair of binoculars.	Egy távcsövet kérnék.	æd^y taavchurvæt kayrnayk
How much do I owe you?	Mennyivel tartozom?	mæn^yeevæl tortawzawm

Reference section

Hungarian cities

Budapest	boodoppæsht
Debrecen	dæbrætsæn
Győr	d^yūrr
Pécs	paych
Szeged	sægæd

Countries

Austria	Ausztria	ooostreeo
Belgium	Belgium	bælgheeoom
Canada	Kanada	konnoddo
Czechoslovakia	Csehszlovákia	chæhslawvaakeeo
East Germany	Német Demokratikus Köztársaság	naymæt dæmawkrottee-koosh kurztaarshoshaag
England	Anglia	ongleeo
Finland	Finnország	feenawrsaag
France	Franciaország	frontseeo-awrsaag
Great Britain	Nagybritánia	nod^ybreetaaneeo
Hungary	Magyarország	mod^yorawrsaag
Ireland	Írország	ēērawrsaag
Italy	Olaszország	eezroæl
Japan	Japán	yoppaan
Netherlands	Hollandia	hawl-londeeo
New Zealand	Újzéland	ōō^yzaylond
Poland	Lengyelország	lænd^yelawrsaag
Scotland	Skócia	shkāwtseeo
Soviet Union	Szovjetunió	sawvyætooneeāw
Sweden	Svédország	svaydawrsaag
Switzerland	Svájc	shvaa^yts
United States	Egyesült Államok	æd^yæshewlt aal-lommawk
Wales	Vélsz	væls
West Germany	Nyugatnémetország	n^yoogotnaymætawrsaawg
Yugoslavia	Jugoszlávia	yoogawslaaveeo

... and continents

Africa	Afrika	ofreeko
Asia	Ázsia	aazheeo
Australia	Ausztrália	ooostraaleeo
Europe	Európa	æoorāwpo
North America	Északamerika	ayssokkommæreeko
South America	Délamerika	daylommæreeko

Numbers

0	nulla	nool-lo
1	egy	æd^y
2	kettő	kæt-tūr
3	három	haarawm
4	négy	nayd^y
5	öt	urt
6	hat	hot
7	hét	hayt
8	nyolc	n^{y}awlts
9	kilenc	keelænts
10	tíz	tēēz
11	tizenegy	teezænæd^y
12	tizenkettő	teezænkæt-tūr
13	tizenhárom	teezænhaarawm
14	tizennégy	teezæn-nayd^y
15	tizenöt	teezænurt
16	tizenhat	teezænhot
17	tizenhét	teezænhayt
18	tizennyolc	teezæn-n^{y}awlts
19	tizenkilenc	teezænkeelænts
20	húsz	hōōss
21	huszonegy	hoossawnæd^y
22	huszonkettő	hoossawnkæt-tūr
23	huszonhárom	hoossawnhaarawm
24	huszonnégy	hoossawn-nayd^y
25	huszonöt	hoossawnurt
26	huszonhat	hoossawnhot
27	huszonhét	hoossawnhayt
28	huszonnyolc	hoossawn-n^{y}awlts
29	huszonkilenc	hoossawnkeelænts
30	harminc	hormeents
31	harmincegy	hormeentsæd^y
32	harminckettő	hormeentskæt-tūr
33	harminchárom	hormeentshaarawm
40	negyven	næd^{y}væn
41	negyvenegy	næd^{y}vænæd^y
42	negyvenkettő	næd^{y}vænkæt-tūr
43	negyvenhárom	næd^{y}vænhaarawm
50	ötven	urtvæn
51	ötvenegy	urtvænæd^y
52	ötvenkettő	urtvænkæt-tūr
53	ötvenhárom	urtvænhaarawm
60	hatvan	hotvon
61	hatvanegy	hotvonnæd^y

62	hatvankettő	hotvonkæt-tūr
63	hatvanhárom	hotvonhaarawm
70	hetven	hætvæn
71	hetvenegy	hætvænæd[y]
72	hetvenkettő	hætvænkæt-tūr
73	hetvenhárom	hætvænhaarawm
80	nyolcvan	n[y]awltsvon
81	nyolcvanegy	n[y]awltsvonnæd[y]
82	nyolcvankettő	n[y]awltsvonkæt-tūr
83	nyolcvanhárom	n[y]awltsvonhaarawm
90	kilencven	keelæntsvæn
91	kilenvenegy	keelæntsvænæd[y]
92	kilencvenkettő	keelæntsvænkæt-tūr
93	kilencvenhárom	keelæntsvænhaarawm
100	egyszáz	æd[y]saaz
101	százegy	saazæd[y]
102	százkettő	saazkæt-tūr
103	százhárom	saazhaarawm
110	száztíz	saaztēēz
120	százhúsz	saazhōōss
130	százharminc	saazhormeents
140	száznegyven	saaznæd[y]væn
150	százötven	saazurtvæn
160	százhatvan	saazhotvon
170	százhetven	saazhætvæn
180	száznyolcvan	saazn[y]awltsvon
190	százkilencven	saazkeelæntsvæn
200	kettőszáz	kæt-tūrsaaz
300	háromszáz	haarawmsaaz
400	négyszáz	nayd[y]saaz
500	ötszáz	urtsaaz
600	hatszáz	hotsaaz
700	hétszáz	haytsaaz
800	nyolcszáz	n[y]awlts-saaz
900	kilencszáz	keelænts-saaz
1000	egyezer	æd[y]æzær
1100	ezeregyszáz	æzæræd[y]saaz
1200	ezerkettőszáz	æzærkæt-tūrsaaz
1300	ezerháromszáz	æzærhaarawmsaaz
2000	kétezer	kaytæzær
5000	ötezer	urtæzær
10,000	tízezer	tēēzæzær
50,000	ötvenezer	urtvænæzær
100,000	százezer	saazæzær
1,000,000	egymillió	æd[y]meel-leeāw

first	első	ælshūr
second	második	maashawdeek
third	harmadik	hormoddeek
fourth	negyedik	næd^{V}ædeek
fifth	ötödik	urturdeek
sixth	hatodik	hottawdeek
seventh	hetedik	hætædeek
eighth	nyolcadik	n^{V}awltsoddeek
ninth	kilencedik	keelæntsædeek
tenth	tizedik	teezædeek
hundredth	századik	saazoddeek
thousandth	ezredik	æzrædeek
once	egyszer	æd^{V}sær
twice	kétszer	kaytsær
three times	háromszor	haarawmsawr
half	fél	fayl
half of ...	a ... fele	o ... fælæ
a quarter	egy negyed	æd^V næd^{V}æd
a third	egy harmad	æd^V hormod
a pair of ...	egy pár ...	æd^V paar
a dozen	egy tucat	æd^V tootsot
half a dozen	féltucat	fayltootsot
the 19th century	a tizenkilencedik század	o teezækeelæntsædeek saazod
in the 20th century	a huszadik században	o hoossoddeek saazodbon
How old are you?	Hány éves?	haan^V ayvæsh
I'm 26.	26 éves vagyok.	26 ayvæsh vod^{V}awk
When's your birthday?	Mikor van a születésnapja?	meekawr von o sewlætayshnopyo
I was born in ...	...-ban/-ben születtem.	...-bon/-bæn sewlættæm
1981	ezerkilencszáznyolcvanegy	æzærkeelæntssaazn^{V}awltsvonæd^V
1982	ezerkilencszáznyolcvankettő	æzærkeelæntssaazn^{V}awltsvonkæt-tūr
1983	ezerkilencszáznyolcvanhárom	æzærkeelæntssaazn^{V}awltsvonhaarawm
1984	ezerkilencszáznyolcvannégy	æzærkeelæntssaazn^{V}awltsvonnayd^V

Time

**tizenkettő óra múlt
tizenöt perccel**
(teezænkæt-tūr a̅w̅ro
mo̅o̅lt teezænurt
pærts-tsæl)

**egy óra múlt húsz
perccel**
(æd^y a̅w̅ro mo̅o̅lt
ho̅o̅ss pærts-tsæl)

fél négy*
(fayl nayd^y)

**négy óra harmincöt
perc**
(nayd^y a̅w̅ro hormeen-
tsurt pærts)

**hat óra lesz húsz
perc múlva**
(hot a̅w̅ro læs ho̅o̅ss
pærts mo̅o̅lvo)

háromnegyed hét
(haarawmnæd^yæd
hayt)

**öt perc múlva
kilenc óra**
(urt pærts mo̅o̅lvo
keelænts a̅w̅ro)

tíz óra
(te̅e̅z a̅w̅ro)

**tizenegy óra múlt
öt perccel**
(teezænæd^y a̅w̅ro mo̅o̅lt
urt pærts-tsæl)

---

* literally "half *to* four".

mid-night | 11 p.m. | 10 p.m. | 9 p.m. | 8 p.m. | 7 p.m. | 6 p.m. | 5 p.m. | 4 p.m. | 3 p.m. | 2 p.m. | 1 p.m. | noon | 11 a.m. | 10 a.m. | 9 a.m. | 8 a.m. | 7 a.m. | 6 a.m. | 5 a.m. | 4 a.m. | 3 a.m. | 2 a.m. | 1 a.m.

Date Line

Eastern European Time
Central European Time
Western European Time (G.M.T.)

Atlantic Time
Eastern Time
Central Time
Mountain Time
Pacific Time
Alaska Time

Countries which have adopted a time differing from that in the corresponding time zone. Note that also in the USSR, official time is one hour ahead of the time in each corresponding time zone. In summer, numerous countries advance time one hour ahead of standard time.

REFERENCE SECTION

When?

What time is it?	Hány óra?	haan^y a̅w̅ro
It's ...	... óra van.	... a̅w̅ro von
Excuse me. Can you tell me the time?	Bocsánat. Megmondaná hogy hány óra van?	bawchaanot. mægmawndonnaa hawd^y haan^y a̅w̅ro von
At what time does ... open?	Mikor nyit a/az ...?	meekawr n^yeet zaar o/oz
At what time does ... close?	Mikor zár be a/az ...?	meekawr zaar bæ o/oz
At what time does it begin?	Mikor kezdődik?	meekawr kæzdu̅r̅deek
At what time does it end?	Mikor van vége?	meekawr von vaygæ
I'll meet you at ... tomorrow.	Holnap ... órakor találkozunk.	hawlnop ... a̅w̅rokkawr tollaalkawzoonk
At what time will you be there?	Mikor lesz ott?	meekawr læs awt
At what time should I be there?	Mikorra jöjjek?	meekawr-ro yur^y-yæk
Can I come at ...?	Jöhetek ... -kor?	yurhætæk ...-kawr
9 o'clock	9-kor	9-kawr
half past 2	fél-3-kor	fayl 3-kawr
I'm sorry, I'm late.	Sajnálom, hogy elkéstem.	shoynaalawm hawd^y ælkayshtæm
after	utánna	ootaan-no
before	előtte	ælu̅rt-tæ
early	korán	kawraan
on time	pontosan	pawntawshon
in time	időben	eedu̅rbæn
late	későn	kayshu̅rn
noon/midnight	délben/éjfélkor	daylbæn/ay^yfaylkawr
hour	egy óra	æd^y a̅w̅ro
half an hour	félóra	faylaw̅ro
quarter of an hour	egy negyed óra	æd^y næd^yæd a̅w̅ro
minute	perc	pærts
second	másodperc	maashawdpærts

Days

What day is it today?	**Ma milyen nap van?**	mo mee^yæn nop von
It's ...	**... van.**	... von
Sunday	**Vasárnap***	voshaarnop
Monday	**Hétfő**	haytfūr
Tuesday	**Kedd**	kæd
Wednesday	**Szerda**	særdo
Thursday	**Csütörtök**	chewturrturk
Friday	**Péntek**	payntæk
Saturday	**Szombat**	sawmbot
in the morning	**reggel**	ræg-gæl
at noon	**délben**	daylbæn
in the afternoon	**délután**	daylootaan
in the evening	**este**	æshtæ
at night	**éjjel**	ay^y-yæl
at midnight	**éjfélkor**	ay^yfaylkawr
the day before yesterday	**tegnapelőtt**	tægnopælūrt
yesterday	**tegnap**	tægnop
today	**ma**	mo
tomorrow	**holnap**	hawlnop
the day after tomorrow	**holnapután**	hawlnoppootaan
the day before	**az előző nap**	oz ælūrzūr nop
the next day	**a következő nap**	o kurvætkæzūr nop
two days ago	**két nappal ezelőtt**	kayt nop-pol æzælūrt
in three days' time	**három nap múlva**	haarawm nop mōolvo
last week	**a múlt héten**	o mōolt haytæn
this week	**ezen a héten**	æzæn o haytæn
next week	**a jövő héten**	o yurvūr haytæn
birthday	**születésnap**	sewlætayshnop
day	**nap**	nop
holiday	**ünnepnap**	ewn-næpnop
holidays	**szabadság**	sobbodshaag
month	**hónap**	hāwnop
week	**hét**	hayt
week-end	**hétvége**	haytvaygæ
working day	**munkanap**	moonkonnop
year	**év**	ayv

REFERENCE SECTION

---

* Note that, except when they appear at the beginning of a sentence, the names of days and months are not capitalized in Hungarian.

Months

January	január*	yonnooaar
February	február	fæbrooaar
March	március	martseeoosh
April	április	aapreeleesh
May	május	maa^yoosh
June	június	yōōneeoosh
July	július	yōōleeoosh
August	augusztus	ooogoostoosh
September	szeptember	sæptæmbær
October	október	awktāwbær
November	november	nawvvæmbær
December	december	dætsæmbær

since June	június óta	yōōneeoosh āwto
in August	augusztusban	ooogoostooshbon
3 months ago	3 hónappal ezelőtt	3 hawnop-pol æzælūrt
last month	a múlt hónapban	o mōōlt hawnopbon
next month	a következő hónapban	o kurvætkæzūr hawnop-bon
the month before	az előző hónapban	oz ælūrzūr hawnopbon
the following month	a következő hónapban	o kurvætkæzūr hawnopbon

Letter headings are written thus:

Budapest, May 24, 1981   **Budapest 1981 május 24**

Seasons

spring	tavasz	tovvoss
summer	nyár	n^yaar
autumn	ősz	ūrss
winter	tél	tayl

in spring	tavasszal	tovvos-sol
in summer	nyáron	n^yaarawn
in autumn	ősszel	ūrs-sæl
in winter	télen	taylæn

---

* Note that the names of days and months are not capitalized in Hungarian.

Public holidays

January 1	**Újév**	New Year's Day
April 4	**A felszabadulás ünnepe**	Liberation Day
May 1	**A munka ünnepe**	Labour Day
August 20	**Az alkotmány napja**	Constitution Day
November 7	**A forradalom ünnepe**	Revolution Day
December 25	**Karácsony első napja**	Christmas Day
December 26	**Karácsony második napja**	Boxing Day
Movable:	**Húsvét hétfő**	Easter Monday

The year round

Here are the average monthly temperatures in Fahrenheit and centigrade for some centres in Hungary:

	Budapest		Lake Balaton		Mountains	
	°F	°C	°F	°C	°F	°C
January	34	1	37	3	18	− 8
February	34	1	32	0	14	−10
March	46	8	48	9	32	0
April	52	11	55	13	43	6
May	59	15	61	16	50	10
June	66	19	68	20	57	14
July	68	20	75	24	59	15
August	66	19	73	23	55	13
September	61	16	64	18	50	10
October	54	12	59	15	48	9
November	37	3	45	7	28	− 2
December	36	2	39	4	21	− 6

Common abbreviations

áll.	állami	state
ált.	általános	general
bek.	bekezdés	paragraph
B.N.V.	Budapesti Nemzetközi Vásár	Budapest International Fair
Bp.	Budapest	Budapest
db/drb.	darab	piece
d.e.	délelőtt	a.m.
d.u.	délután	p.m.
et.	elvtárs	comrade
évf.	évfolyam	year
f.é.	folyó év	this year
f.h.	folyó hó	this month
fmh	feltételes megállóhely	request stop
főv.	fővárosi	metropolitan
fsz.	földszint	ground floor
gk.	gépkocsi	car
gy.v.	gyorsvonat	express train
hat.eng.	hatóságilag engedélyezett	licensed
IBUSZ	Idegenforgalmi Hiv.	Ibusz Tourist Agency
kb.	körülbelül	approximately
K.B.	Központi Bizottság	Central Committee
KEOKH	Külföldieket Ellenőrző Országos Központ	Foreigners' Registration Office
Közért	élelmiszerüzlet	food shop trust
LE	lóerő	horsepower
MALÉV	Magyar Légiforgalmi Vállalat	Hungarian Airlines
MÁV	Magyar Államvasutak	Hungarian State Railways
M.N.B.	Magyar Nemzeti Bank	Hungarian National Bank
M.T.I.	Magyar Távirati Iroda	Hungarian Telegraphic Services
p.u.	pályaudvar	railway station
röv.	rövidítés	abbreviation
s.k.	sajátkezüleg	in one's own hand
stb.	és a többi	etc.
szt.	szent	saint
távb.	telefon	telephone
T.c.	Tisztelt Cím!	Sir, Madam (polite, written)
u.	utca, út	street
u.a.	ugyanaz	the same, idem
u.n.	úgynevezett	so called
v.á.	vasútállomás	railway station

Conversion tables

Centimetres and inches

To change centimetres into inches, multiply by .39.

To change inches into centimetres, multiply by 2.54.

	in.	feet	yards
1 mm	0.039	0.003	0.001
1 cm	0.39	0.03	0.01
1 dm	3.94	0.32	0.10
1 m	39.40	3.28	1.09

	mm	cm	m
1 in.	25.4	2.54	0.025
1 ft.	304.8	30.48	0.305
1 yd.	914.4	91.44	0.914

(32 metres = 35 yards)

Temperature

To convert centigrade into degrees Fahrenheit, multiply centigrade by 1.8 and add 32.

To convert degrees Fahrenheit into centigrade, subtract 32 from Fahrenheit and divide by 1.8.

Metres and feet

The figure in the middle stands for both metres and feet, e.g., 1 metre = 3.28 ft. and 1 foot = 0.30 m.

Metres		Feet
0.30	1	3.281
0.61	2	6.563
0.91	3	9.843
1.22	4	13.124
1.52	5	16.403
1.83	6	19.686
2.13	7	22.967
2.44	8	26.248
2.74	9	29.629
3.05	10	32.810
3.35	11	36.091
3.66	12	39.372
3.96	13	42.635
4.27	14	45.934
4.57	15	49.215
4.88	16	52.496
5.18	17	55.777
5.49	18	59.058
5.79	19	62.339
6.10	20	65.620
7.62	25	82.023
15.24	50	164.046
22.86	75	246.069
30.48	100	328.092

REFERENCE SECTION

Other conversion charts

Weight conversion

The figure in the middle stands for both kilograms and pounds, e.g., 1 kilogram = 2.205 lb. and 1 pound = 0.45 kilograms.

Kilograms (kg.)		Avoirdupois pounds
0.45	1	2.205
0.91	2	4.409
1.36	3	6.614
1.81	4	8.818
2.27	5	11.023
2.72	6	13.227
3.17	7	15.432
3.62	8	17.636
4.08	9	19.841
4.53	10	22.045
6.80	15	33.068
9.06	20	44.089
11.33	25	55.113
22.65	50	110.225
34.02	75	165.338
45.30	100	220.450

NORTH
ÉSZAK
(ayssok)

WEST
NYUGAT
(nᵛoogot)

EAST
KELET
(kælæt)

SOUTH
DÉL
(dayl)

REFERENCE SECTION

What does that sign mean?

You're sure to encounter some of these signs or notices on your trip:

A bejáratot kérjük szabadon hagyni	Do not block the entrance
Átjárás tilos	Trespassers will be prosecuted
Bejárat	Entrance
Belépés díjtalan	Admission free
Dohányzó	Smoking allowed
Eladó	For sale
Elfogyott	Sold out
Érintése tilos	Do not touch
Fáradjon be	Enter without knocking
Fel	Up
Felvilágosítás	Information
Férfi W.C.	Men's toilets
Foglalt	Reserved, occupied
Forró	Hot
Halálveszély	Danger of death
Hideg	Cold
Húzni	Pull
Kérem, csengessen	Please ring
Kiadó	To let
Kiárusítás	Sale
Kijárat	Exit
Le	Down
Magánterület	Private
Magánút	Private road
Női W.C.	Ladies' toilets
Nyitva	Open
Pénztáros	Cash desk
Szabad	Vacant
... kiadó	... for hire (to rent)
Szemetelni tilos	No littering
... tilos	... prohibited
Tilos a belépés	No entry
Tilos a dohányzás	No smoking
Tolni	Push
Várjon kérem	Please wait
Veszély	Danger
Vészkijárat	Emergency exit
Vigyázat	Caution
Vigyázat! Harapós kutya	Beware of the dog
Zárva	Closed

Emergency

By the time the emergency is upon you it's too late to turn to this page to find the Hungarian for "Call the police". So have a look at this short list beforehand—and, if you want to be on the safe side, learn the expressions shown in capitals.

Be quick	Gyorsan	d^yawrshon
Call the police	Hívja a rendőrséget	hēēvyo o rændūrrshaygæt
CAREFUL	ÓVATOSAN	āwvottawshon
Come here	Jöjjön ide	yur^y-yurn eedæ
Come in	Szabad	sobbod
Consulate	Konzulátus	kawnzoolaatoosh
Danger	Veszély	væsay^y
Embassy	Nagykövetség	nod^ykurvætshayg
FIRE	TŰZ	tēwz
GET A DOCTOR	HÍVJON ORVOST	hēēvyawn awrvawsht
Get help quickly	Hozzon gyorsan segítséget	hawz-zon d^yawrshon shæghēētshaygæt
Go away	Távozzék	taavawz-zayk
HELP	SEGÍTSÉG	shæghēētshayg
I'm ill	Beteg vagyck	bætæg vod^yawk
I'm lost	Eltévedtem	æltayvædtæm
Keep your hands to yourself	Ne fogdosson	næ fawgdawsh-shawn
Leave me alone	Hagyjon békét	hod^yyawn baykayt
Lie down	Feküdjön le	fækewdyurn læ
Listen	Figyeljen	feed^yælyæn
Look	Nézzen körül	nayz-zæn kurrewl
Look out	Vigyázat	veed^yaazot
POLICE	RENDŐRSÉG	rændūrrshayg
STOP	MEGÁLLNI	mægaalnee
Stop, or I'll scream	Hagyjon békét, vagy kiáltok	hod^yawn baykayt vod^y keeaaltawk
Stop that man	Állítsák meg azt az embert	aal-lēētshaak mæg ost oz æmbært
STOP THIEF	FOGJÁK MEG TOLVAJ	fawgyaak mæg tawlvoy

REFERENCE SECTION

Emergency telephone numbers:		
Ambulance	04	**Mentők**
Fire	05	**Tűzoltók**
Police	07	**Rendőrség**

CAR ACCIDENTS: see page 150

Index

INDEX

Quick reference page

Yes/No.	Igen/Nem.	eegæn/næm
Please.	Kérem.	kayræm
Thank you.	Köszönöm.	kursurnurm
Excuse me.	Bocsásson meg.	bawchaash-shawn mæg
I'm sorry.	Sajnálom.	shoynaalawn
Waiter/Waitress, please!	Pincér/Pincérnő, kérem!	peentsayr/peentsayrnūr kayræm
How much is that?	Mennyibe kerül?	mæn^{y}eebæ kærewl
Where are the toilets?	Hol a W.C.?	hawl o vaytsay

Toilets	
FÉRFI W.C. (fayrfee vaytsay)	NŐI W.C. (nūŕee vaytsay)

Please, could you tell me ...?	Kérem, meg tudná mondani, hogy ...?	kayræm mæg toodnaa mawndonnee hawd^y
where/when/why	hol/mikor/miért	hawl/meekawr/meèayrt
What time is it?	Hány óra van?	haan^y aẁro von
Help me, please.	Segítene kérem.	shægheètænæ kayræm
Where's the ... consulate/embassy?	Hol ... Konzulátus/ Nagykövetség?	hawl ... kawnzoolaatoosh/ nod^{y}kurvætshayg
American	az amerikai	oz ommæreeko-ee
British	az angol	oz ongawl
Canadian	a kanadai	o konnoddo-ee
What does this mean?	Ez mit jelent?	æz meet yælænt
I don't understand.	Nem értem.	næm ayrtæm
Do you speak English?	Beszél angolul?	bæsayl ongawlool